SWEAT OF THE SUN, TEARS OF THE MOON: | GOLD AND EMERALD TREASURES OF COLOMBIA

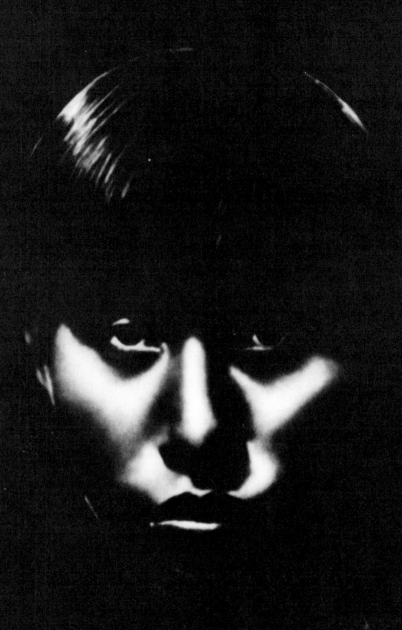

TERRA MAGAZINE
PUBLICATIONS
Dorothy Halle Seligman, Editor
Natural History Museum Alliance
of Los Angeles County
Los Angeles, California

SWEAT OF THE SUN, TEARS OF THE MOON: GOLD AND EMERALD TREASURES OF COLOMBIA

The Natural History Museum of Los Angeles County
July 4–September 6, 1981

Essays by:

PETER T. FURST, PhD
Professor of Anthropology
State University of New York,
Albany

PETER C. KELLER, PhD
Director of Education
Gemological Institute of America
Santa Monica, California

WILLIAM B. LEE, PhD
Director
Natural History Museum of
Los Angeles County
and
KENNETH RUDDLE, PhD
National Museum of Ethnology
Osaka, Japan

G. REICHEL-DOLMATOFF, PhD
Professor of Anthropology
University of California
at Los Angeles

RICHARD EVANS SCHULTES, PhD
Professor of Botany
Director, Harvard Botanical Museum
Harvard University
Cambridge, Massachusetts
and
ALEC BRIGHT
Exhibit Designer
Museo del Oro
Banco de la República
Bogotá, Colombia

Introduction by
LUIS DUQUE GÓMEZ, PhD
Director, Museo del Oro
Banco de la República
Bogotá, Colombia

Plate captions by
WARWICK M. BRAY, PhD
Pre-History Department
Institute of Archaeology
University of London

Color photography by
HAROLD and ERICA VAN PELT

3

Published in conjunction with the Exhibition, *Sweat of the Sun, Tears of the Moon: Gold and Emerald Treasures of Colombia*, held at The Natural History Museum of Los Angeles County, July 4–September 6, 1981.

The exhibition was made possible by grants from Avianca Airlines, the Colombian international airlines; Federación Nacional de Cafeteros (Coffee Federation of Colombia); and Galeria Cano. The catalog received grants from Corporación Nacional de Turismo-Colombia (Colombian National Tourist Office); Willis F. Bronkie, Cia., Ltd., Greenfire® Emeralds of Colombia; Robert P. Miller Jr.; and Hotchkis Foundation. Funds for the poster designed by Saul Bass/Herb Yager & Associates were provided by Kawai Ltd., Emeralds of Colombia.

Exhibition organized by William B. Lee, Director, Natural History Museum of Los Angeles County and Peter C. Keller.
Exhibition designed by Alec Bright, Exhibition Designer, Museo del Oro, Bogotá.
Honorary Curator for the Exhibition: Señora Clara Muñoz de Yust.

The color photographs, made especially for this exhibition, were taken in Colombia and Los Angeles by Harold and Erica Van Pelt. The "Patricia" emerald photograph on p. 52 is courtesy of the American Museum of Natural History, New York; the "Hooker" emerald and "the Inquisition Necklace" photographs on pp. 54–55 are courtesy of the National Museum of Natural History, Smithsonian Institution, Washington, D.C.; mining scenes on pp. 9, 35, 36, 51 and 55 are courtesy of Peter C. Keller.

The article, *Ancient Gold Pectorals from Colombia: Mushroom Effigies?*, has been adapted from the *Boletin del Oro* (Banco de la República) Ano. 3, Bogotá, Colombia, and *Botanical Museum Leaflets*, Harvard University, May–June, 1979, Vol. 27, Nos. 5–6; *El Dorado: Colombia's Golden Heritage* has been adapted from a booklet with permission from the authors. The color plate captions have been adapted from *The Gold of El Dorado* by Dr. Warwick Bray.

Copyright © 1981 by TERRA Magazine Publications
Natural History Museum Alliance, Publisher
Dorothy Halle Seligman, Editor in Chief and Supervisor
Kilbee Cormack Brittain, Assistant Editor

Harry Pack, Tri-Arts, Designer
Mary Butler, Detail map of Colombia
Aimee Siefried, Production aide

Contents

Preface

In the summer of 1978, the international price of gold began to increase at a remarkable rate, eventually culminating in the highest prices that have ever been paid for this precious metal. Perhaps this was due to the instability of the international monetary systems or the insecurity of world politics. But whatever the reason, the value of gold once again reflected an ancient respect for this dearest of metals which, even in an age of electronic currency, still symbolizes an eternal and lasting source of wealth.

It was at about this time that several independent ideas came together in Los Angeles, whose end result is this exhibition at the Natural History Museum, "Sweat of the Sun, Tears of the Moon: Gold and Emerald Treasures of Colombia."

Consul of Colombia in Los Angeles Señora Clara Muñoz de Yust had for many years wanted to bring to Los Angeles an exhibition from the magnificent Museo del Oro in Bogotá. I had been fascinated by the Gold Museum and the wonderful complex of Andean legends and traditions which revolved around gold and its symbolic value to the ancient peoples of the New World. An acquaintance of mine since the early 1970's, Alec Bright, the Exhibit Designer of the Museo del Oro in Bogotá, passed through Los Angeles that year transporting a remarkable collection from Colombia to be exhibited at the Royal Academy in London. The idea was spawned to organize a magnificent collection of pre-Columbian gold for Los Angeles from the beautiful and mysterious land of Colombia, the hub of goldworking traditions in the New World. Yet another concept entered the picture at this point when Dr. Peter Keller, then curator of gems and mineralogy at the Natural History Museum of Los Angeles County, returned from an extensive documentary project involving research on Colombian emeralds. The idea of creating an exhibition which would highlight the two most significant aspects of pre-Columbian wealth in this region began to be formulated.

Throughout the folklore of the New World peoples, (and indeed on a worldwide basis) a recurring theme emerges which explains the source of precious elements, both metals and crystals. The most recurrent of these themes attributes these prized and beautiful elements to gifts from the gods, whomever those dieties might be. In all of the ancient religions the most visible and dominant elements in the heavens are the sun, the moon, and the stars. The most commonly recurring theme in world mythology when speaking of the source of gold attributes the glistening yellow metal, as everlasting and predictable as the dawning of each new day, to the sun. To all of the Andean peoples who worshipped the sun, its most visible presence on earth was gold. In the same way, the vibrant, cool emerald crystals which emerged from the earth in the most unexpected and unusual places also represented heavenly elements and, at least to the Muzo people of Colombia's northern Andes, these lovely crystaline stones were the tears of the moon. The sources of these beautiful legends are conjectural; what's *important* is that they are universal and that anyone who reflects on the metaphorical image suggested by the sweat of the sun and the tears of the moon is moved. We have taken the liberty of using this widespread Andean metaphor to convey the feeling of the exhibition of gold and emeralds from their most significant source, Colombia.

Colombia's Indian rituals combine the sacred myths of golden treasures and precious emeralds. The Natural History Museum's exhibition is the first time these two important minerals have been joined together within an ethnological context for purposes beyond mere beauty. We have endeavored, both in the exhibition and in this catalog, to shed some light on the importance of the objects to the Indians for their ritual or shamanistic rather than material values—and to re-emphasize the universal appeal of these precious elements.

William B. Lee

Director, Natural History Museum of Los Angeles County

Woodcut from La Historia General y Natural de las Indias *by Gonzalo Fernández de Oviedo y Valdés, 1535–48.*

Acknowledgments

This exhibition has been made possible by grants from Avianca Airlines, the Colombian International Airlines; Galeria Cano; and Federacíon Nacional de Cafeteros (Coffee Federation of Colombia). The catalog has been funded by Willis F. Bronkie, Cia, Ltd., Greenfire Emeralds of Colombia, Limited; Corporacíon Nacional de Turismo-Colombia (Colombian National Tourist Office); Robert P. Miller Jr.; and Hotchkis Foundation. Funds for the poster, designed by Saul Bass/Herb Yager & Associates especially for this exhibit, were provided by Kawai Ltd., Emeralds of Colombia.

The exhibition is the cumulative effort of many individuals. From Colombia we have had the most magnificent cooperation imaginable. Dr. Luis Duque Gómez, director of the Museo del Oro, Banco de la República, Bogotá, has encouraged our effort from the first moments of conception. His help and insight have made the exhibition not only possible but unequalled. We are indebted to him for his museum's loan of more than 500 gold and pottery objects. Dr. Rafael Gama, Director General of the Banco de la República which supports the Museo del Oro, has made it possible for us to borrow five huge emerald crystals from the bank's collections which have never been exhibited anywhere in the world before. Alec Bright who is an architect by training but an anthropologist in his heart, has given valuable advice and his professional eye for design.

Without the untiring efforts and persistence of Señora Clara Muñoz de Yust, Consul of Colombia at Los Angeles, the dream of this exhibit would never have become a reality. Her enthusiasm for the project fired the enthusiasm of her friends in Colombia, and her dynamism kept the project alive. Her brother in Colombia, Juan Jacobo Muñoz Delgado, Minister of Social Welfare, deserves our special thanks for his assistance with the arrangements for the exhibition. And particular accolades go to Señora Nydia Quintero de Turbay, wife of the president of Colombia, and to Señora Helena Tamayo de Muñoz. Dr. Alvaro Cala, president of Avianca Airlines, was a great help, always ready when we needed him, as was Jairo Sanabria, manager, Los Angeles office of Avianca.

In the final analysis, an exhibition is only as great as the objects on display. We have been successful in securing an unprecedented number of items for this exhibit which have never been shown together before, and many which have never been shared by any audience. In addition to the loans from the Museo del Oro and the Banco de la República, we are grateful for objects from the Museo Arqueologico del Banco Popular, Bogotá; the Museo Nacional, Bogotá; and a number of private lenders of Colombia. They include Señor Guillermo Cano Mejia of Galeria Cano who loaned several gold and emerald objects, plus the only pre-Columbian emerald known to have been worked by natives; Dr. Hernán Borrero Urrutia; Señor Jaime Errazuriz; Alec Bright; Kawai Ltd., Emeralds of Colombia; and Willis F. Bronkie, Cia, Ltd., Greenfire Emeralds of Colombia.

The exhibition is enhanced by loans from major American museums. We wish to thank the American Museum of Natural History for the famous "Patricia" emerald; the Smithsonian Institution for the extraordinary "Inquisition Necklace," and the brilliant "Hooker" and "Gachalá" emeralds; the University Museum, University of Pennsylvania, for a considerable number of fine gold objects; the Field Museum, Chicago, for five outstanding gold artifacts.

Private lenders whose objects grace this exhibit include Allan Caplan, Ed N. Harrison, Dr. Warwick Bray, and M. S. Sater & Co., Inc., Beverly Hills, California.

The exhibition has been superbly designed by Alec Bright. Frank Ackerman, Chief of Exhibitions at the Natural History Museum of Los Angeles County, and his staff have performed miracles, compounded of talent and extraordinary hard work. Dr. Anthony Kampf, curator of mineralogy, has worked tirelessly. And we are particularly grateful to Leon G. Arnold, Assistant Director, for his frank and honest critique of the project at each important step along the way. Within the exhibits we are grateful to John F. McCaughin of J. F. McCaughin Co. for providing samples of modern investment casting processes.

The steady hand of William W. Drewry Jr., chairman of the Natural History Museum Foundation, was always appreciated; W. Stuart Ritter, executive vice-president, Natural History Museum Foundation, has been a part of the major planning team and an important asset. The Board of Supervisors of Los Angeles County and its chief administrative officer, Harry L. Hufford, the Natural History Museum Board of Governors, and the Natural History Museum Foundation trustees all deserve votes of thanks. The Natural History Museum Alliance, under its chairman, Mrs. David Duque, has offered strong support and is the publisher of the catalog.

The director's secretary, Patricia Reynolds, has performed with calm, unflappable efficiency at all times; Myra Hester, Registrar, has recorded and watched over every item; Delbert Souza has supervised security; Robin Simpson, Joan Grasty, and Kathy Donahue have performed on a special invaluable committee; Judy Astone and her Docents have supplemented publicity for the exhibition. Frances S. Kellough, Administrative Secretary, Natural History Museum Alliance, has performed in her usual outstanding fashion. Shelly Stephens and Marion Harris have selected merchandise and publications which will enhance the Ethnic Arts Shop during the exhibition.

The catalog has been meticulously edited and supervised by Dorothy Halle Seligman. She has been ably assisted by Kilbee Cormack Brittain and Robin Simpson. It has been designed by Harry Pack/Tri-Arts, and objects in the catalog were photographed with consummate skill, love, and attention to detail by Harold and Erica Van Pelt.

William B. Lee, *Director*

Introduction

El Dorado, in Spanish "the gilded one," was a name applied to the king or chief priest of the Muisca Indians, who was said to cover himself with gold dust at the ceremony of his investiture. This ceremony was held at the sacred lake of Guatavita, high in the Andes, some fifty kilometers north of what is now Bogotá, Colombia.

In the mid-sixteenth century the legend of El Dorado completely captured the imagination of Europeans and induced many Spanish explorers to lead expeditions in search of the treasures they fantasized. These explorers conjured up cities, temples, and even streets paved with resplendent gold. Their wild fancies were encouraged by the cunning native people who were anxious to get the conquering torrent of foreign expeditionaries as far away from their particular tribes as possible.

If one reads the accounts of the El Dorado ceremony recorded by a few Spanish chroniclers, one finds that emeralds were just as important as gold to the Muisca Indians in their ceremonies and beliefs. Thus, it was the combined treacherous and evasive lure of glittering gold and brilliant emeralds which delineated the routes of the European discoverers of the vast territories which today comprise the country of Colombia—and the hunt for that treasure was the principal factor which stimulated the conquest and subjugation of the indigenous groups populating this land.

On the ruins of native cultures newly-founded Spanish towns arose, such as San Sebastian de Urabá and Santa Maria le Antigua del Darién (1509–1514), in order to collect the gold dust which the Indians of Nutibara collected "by basketfuls," according to the exaggerated words of Vasco Nuñez de Balboa. Santa Marta sprang up (1525) to snatch the riches of the gold mines and the sanctuaries of Posigueica and Buritica, evident in the personal ornaments of the Taironas. Cartagena was built in 1533 to plunder the legendary riches of the Sinú tombs, and Santa Fé and Tunja were created between 1538–1539 to grab both the gold cast as offerings to the gods who made their abode in the depths of the lakes, and for the tempting green of the emeralds. And there were Pasto and Popayán (1536–1539), where the treasures extracted from the alluvial rivers flowing down the Pacific slope were concentrated; and Cartago (1540) where the conquerors lusted for the splendid gold jewelry of the Carrapas and Quimbayas; and lastly, Santafé de Antioquia (1541), which was founded near the rich vein source of most of the gold refined by the people of Darien, and which was worked with such skill by the Sinús that their creations were traded to distant lands in Mesoamerica and the Antilles.

The Spanish conquerors took it all, plus the treasures of the Muisca chiefs and priests; the contents of the rich chamber tombs of Finzenú; the plates of hammered gold which covered the wooden sculptures of the same region; the golden armor used in combat by the warriors in the southern part of Antioquia and in northern Caldas and Urabá. With it they not only satisfied the covetous soldiers but also filled the coffers of the distant King of Castile.

There have been many gold shows throughout the world, but this show at the Natural History Museum of Los Angeles County is the first time that emeralds have been shown with the gold to point up their profound religious significance to the Indians. This lovely gem forms part of the origin myth of one of the principal deities, Goranchacha, "child of the sun, born of an emerald." According to a legend told to Padre Simon, our most important seventeenth century chronicler, the following story unfolds:

In ancient times it was announced that the sun would fertilize a maiden from the town of Guachetá and the fruit of her womb would be the true child of the sun king. Hoping for this happening of such grandeur, the chief's daughters often went to the hills near the town in the mornings, hoping to be the chosen one, as did occur. After the term of her pregnancy, the princess gave birth to an emerald, which, kept in her bosom, eventually turned into a beautiful boy, whom she called Goranchacha and who stayed with his mother till he was twenty-four years old. When he was a grown man, the sun's child traveled to the sacred lands of Ramiriquí and Sogamoso to take charge of the tribe. It was Goranchacha's idea to build a great temple to the sun god of Tunja, for the construction of which he began to have large stone blocks collected. But this task was interrupted when news of the arrival of the Spanish expeditionaries on the Atlantic coast was received. At this time the legendary person disappeared forever.

So the emerald was the mythological ancestor of the Muiscas, who lived in the high plateaus of Cundinamarca and Boyaca, and this explains why the aboriginals worked the rich veins of Chivor intensely to procure the magic stone which, together with the gold pieces, was carried by their trade routes to the remotest regions of the land which is today Colombia, and even to neighboring countries.

The treasures which the Museo del Oro and the Banco de la República of Colombia are showing with pride at the Natural History Museum are representative samples which fully prove the evidence of the old chroniclers and historians of conquest times with regard to the fabulous riches of the natives seen by the Spaniards. The Museo del Oro owns nearly 29,000 pieces, skillfully worked by the pre-Columbian master craftsmen, employing an advanced technology rivaling that of modern gold workers. Some of this goldware dates back to the seventh century, and some of it is as late as the end of the sixteenth century, when the goldsmiths' efforts became limited to the exploitation of placer deposits and veins of gold to enrich the exchequer of the Spanish crown. The material in the Museum represents more than two millenniums of continuous work by craftsmen whose masterpieces form a significant part of the cultural heritage of the pre-Columbian Americas. The Museo del

Oro's parent, the Banco de la República, is showing emeralds from its collection, many of which have never before been displayed anywhere. They include five stones ranging in weight from 220 carats to 1796 carats, which are among the largest gem emerald crystals in the world. Mined from the famed Muzo mine of pre-Columbian times between 1947 and 1969, the uncut crystals are natural wonders. We are pleased that our great national treasures are being shared with the people of Los Angeles.

Luis Duque Gómez
Director, Museo del Oro
Banco de la República Colombia
June 1981

The sacred Lake Guatavita today. Many attempts have been made to drain it in order to recover the golden sacrifices. The most intense of recorded attempts was made by Antonio de Sepúlveda, a rich Santa Fe de Bogotá merchant. The deep trench on the left in the picture shows the Sepúlveda cut. He managed to lower the lake by some twenty meters before the cut collapsed. Now the Colombian Government protects Guatavita as part of the nation's historical and cultural heritage.

El Dorado: Colombia's Golden Heritage

by WILLIAM B. LEE and KENNETH RUDDLE

Early man was clearly an artist. The earliest archaeological fragments of simple tools and weapons testify to their makers' desire for beauty of form. From the beginning of metallurgy, gold—an easily-worked, naturally-occurring and unchangeable metal—has been valued as an element most worthy of man's best artistic efforts.

Gold-making in the New World reached an artistic level comparable to that of any other civilization. Gold was worked from Mexico to northern Chile. Sailors, like the Genoese Columbus, in the pay of Spain and seeking a western spice route, found that the land they thought was the Spice Islands was rich in gold. Spices were soon forgotten for the more exciting lure of this valuable metal.

The conquering Europeans found native groups with class structure and specialized craftsmen. Chroniclers have described the golden splendor of the temples and shrines they found in the New World. But for the Indians, the symbolism of gold was ultimately involved with the sun and chieftainship. Chiefs were buried with their gold. Although gold (along with salt, emeralds, maize, and woven cloth) sometimes entered into barter, gold did not have the same economic meaning for the Indians that it has for our western society.

To finance their wars the Spanish conquistadores ransacked the newly-discovered continent, and in an orgy of murder, enslavement, and wanton destruction, seized and melted down the art treasures of the Americas. The coffers of Europe filled with bullion as countless, wondrous objects passed into oblivion.

The gold-crafting people of what is today Colombia produced thousands of objects of gold, copper, and more rarely, platinum and silver during a period of two thousand years, from about 500 B.C. until the Spanish conquest in the first half of the sixteenth century. After the conquest they produced gold bullion which their masters sent to Spain.

Where are the areas from which the pre-Colombian gold came?

These zones have not yet been precisely defined because Colombian archaeology is still in its formative stages. The nine most important areas about which we *do* have some information are described below:

CALIMA

The Cauca River rises near San Agustin and flows between the Central and Western Cordilleras to join the Magdalena shortly before it reaches the sea. Numerous examples of a gold style known as Calima have been found in the region around the middle of the Cauca. The term "Calima" is derived from the River Calima, the headwaters region of which has yielded many pieces of this style. The area forms part of the Cauca valley geographical region.

Most of the goldware found is of high-grade metal. Forms are varied, but perhaps the most notable are the scores of large, oval breastplates adorned with realistic human faces which wear large spool-and-cup ornaments. Many other items worn by the Calima people have been found, including ear-pieces, diadems, in which the decoration combines not only stylized and naturalistic faces but also the heads of alligator-like animals. These headdresses have a profusion of fringe-like pendants and small round pieces wired to the main part. There are flat bracelets, anklets, ceremonial staffs, lip pendants, and gold throwing sticks—in all, a magnificent regalia which, resplendent under the bright Cauca sun, must have been an unforgettable spectacle. All of these pieces are examples of repoussé work, in which thin cast plates were hammered from the back onto a soft surface to complete forms or to add decoration.

Many jewels were cast in solid gold. Heavy, simple, gold nose rings, some of which rattle when shaken, are common. There is also a ceramic death mask that demonstrates how the nose rings were worn. Many long pins or spatulas, with complex beads representing birds, or masked figures hung with numerous objects come from the Calima style zone. Some masks can even be removed to reveal a face beneath.

Map of the Style Zones

Golden *poporos* formed of several pieces of gold pinned or riveted together abound. Some represent men; others depict jaguars. A number of necklaces and pendants are combined with blue, semiprecious stones. As at San Agustin, many gold objects display the jaguar motif in mouths with protruding fangs.

What of the artisans who made these fine objects, and of the people who wore them? We know that they buried their dead in the shaft tombs, because most of the Calima gold comes from them. They also practiced urn burial, using huge, globular, ceramic containers (Figure 1). Their houses were scattered on platforms over the slopes on which they grew corn, and in the light of evening, deepening shadows still reveal their field divisions, paths, and terraces.

Calima pottery is of high quality. Fat, seated, human figures, obese toads, and many double-spouted vessels, some painted and others incised, are common. A snake whistle comes from this zone, as does a delightful kinkajou seated in a characteristic position, tail round its neck and using a paw to remove a seed from between its teeth. One seated figure with a basket on his back smiles as he contentedly chews a wad of coca, visible from the bulge in one cheek (Figure 2).

The Calima people who made these beautiful and often amusing pieces disappeared before the Spaniards arrived, but their culture has been dated, at least in one section of the Cauca valley, to the eleventh to thirteenth centuries A.D.

MUISCA

The Muisca archaeological zone is the best known and the most clearly-defined, perhaps because the Spaniards made their capital in the area, and administered the country from there after the Conquest. The Muiscas, who spoke a Chibchan language, and are often called "Chibchas," were divided into two confederations.

The former homeland of the Muiscas is a cool, high Andean plateau. Nearby lie even higher areas where little grows. Close, too, are warmer levels rich in tropical fruits, cotton, coca, and other products. The Muiscas were agriculturalists who grew maize in ridged fields or terraces on the Andean slopes. Numerous remains of village sites and isolated houses suggest a dense population.

Although many of the tribes surrounding the plateau were hostile, they nevertheless traded with the Muisca. There is no gold in Muisca territory, so it was bartered in exchange for emeralds, salt, and cotton cloth.

Muisca goldworkers were specialists who had high prestige. If one went to work in another village, two men had to be left as hostages against his safe return. Votive offerings *(tunjos)*, tall, thin, flat figures, with a wealth of ornamentation, dress, and arms, are the distinguishing feature of this people's gold working. Warriors, women, babies, houses, and even hammocks were depicted (Figure 3). Offerings were placed in the bellies of ceramic figures and either buried with the dead or thrown into sacred lakes. The most important of these was the Lake of Guatavita. It was there that El Dorado, the Gilded

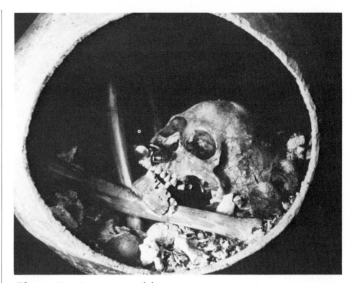

Figure 1. *Contents of funerary urn.*

Figure 2. *Seated human figure carrying basket.*

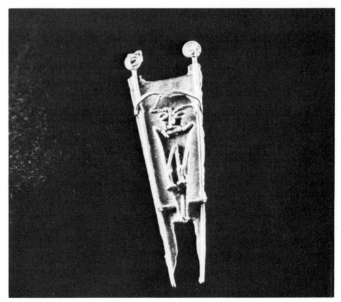

Figure 3. *Votive offering: baby in cradle.*

11

Man, was rowed out on a raft with his attendants at sunrise, to bathe in the icy waters and to wash off the gold dust with which he had been coated until he looked like a resplendent gold statue. As he bathed, his subjects threw golden *tunjos* and emeralds into the lake. This gave rise to the legend of El Dorado, one of the reasons for the conquest of America. Unlike the imaginary Seven Cities of Cibola, El Dorado actually existed.

The Muisca goldsmiths made other ornaments, too. These are better finished than the *tunjos*, which were left as they came from the mold. Other works include large breastplates, round containers, gold throwing sticks, and many pendants hung with round plates. Large rectangular cut-out nosepieces were employed, and are shown on ceramic or gold figures, as are long necklaces worn like bandoliers. When replication of an object was desired, the Muiscas used the lost wax process.

NARIÑO

Nariño, the southernmost of Colombia's Andean gold-working areas, extends into the Carchi region of Ecuador. It is centered on the village of Pupiales and was the home of the Pasto and Quillacinga groups at the time of the Spanish Conquest. It is also the most recently discovered of the archaeological gold-style zones.

Gold pieces are found in the deepest shaft graves known, some descending to fifty feet. The round lateral chamber, dug to one side of the base of the shaft, sometimes has a depression in the center, where the grave goods were deposited. The body or bodies were placed around the sides of the tomb.

The bulk of the goldware consists of thin plate ornaments, with geometric cut-out designs. There are also nosepieces and breastplates decorated with representations of monkeys and birds. Among the heavier pieces are bells and rattles in the form of shells, and golden pan-pipes. A few small gold masks are known, one of which has a bulge in one cheek, showing that these people chewed coca.

An advanced decorative technique, not known from any other part of Colombia, was employed by the Nariño goldsmiths. The surface of gold and copper alloy discs was oxidized over part of its area, in a flowing geometrical pattern, giving the impression of a round plate made from two distinct metals. Some plates were also painted. From this zone comes a large square plate of good quality gold, the heaviest piece yet found in the country. It weighs 2080 gm. (about four lbs.).

Along with these golden pieces, the shaft graves revealed ceramic figurines, pots and ocarinas, stone axes, obsidian points and looking glasses, and cloth woven in ways which differ from the examples found in other parts of Colombia.

Two recently obtained carbon-14 dates indicate that gold-working people occupied the Nariño area during the periods 920 ± 110 years B.P. (Before Present) and 870 ± 120 years B.P. Clarification of the meaning of these data must, however, await more archaeological work in the Nariño Zone.

QUIMBAYA

Focusing on the Central Highlands area of the Quindío and the lower Cauca valley is the gold-working zone known as Quimbaya. Scattered over the slopes of this zone are many cemeteries whose shafts have yielded thousands of heavy, pure gold pieces that are both beautifully designed and perfectly finished. Among the Quimbaya the goldsmith's art reached its highest expression in the Americas.

The Quimbaya zone is now devoted to coffee growing, but in pre-Hispanic times the Quimbaya tribe, and the other groups which must have occupied that land for many centuries, were sedentary cultivators of maize. The chroniclers wrote about the beauty of the landscape, then, as now, green with large traces of giant bamboo.

Quimbaya pottery is well made, and varied, with incised, linear, or punctuated decoration and many examples of negative painting. Painted ceramic figures are characteristic of this zone. Some are flat and solid, with square heads and "coffee bean" eyes, whereas others are modelled in the round, some standing and others seated. Many spindle whorls have been found, as have rollers and stamps, and obsidian looking glasses.

But the abundance and quality of the goldware was the greatest achievement of the Quimbaya people. Large standing figures, adorned with crowns and necklaces, and often holding *poporos* come from this zone. A large *poporo* with a fretted base, and surmounted by four spheres is another Quimbaya masterpiece. This particular lime flask mirrors in gold the gourd *poporos* used by present-day tribes. From this zone, too, come lizards, caymans, eagles, well-burnished and polished necklaces, small decorative masks, and standing figures holding plaques.

One masterwork, the symbolism of which is unknown, depicts masked men carrying two staffs in their hands and wearing double-domed headdresses. These pieces are also found far from the Quimbaya area in the Sinú Zone, and in Panama and Costa Rica, where they were valued as trade pieces.

SAN AGUSTIN AND TIERRADENTRO

In the Colombian massif, the highland region in the south of the country, near the region where the Andes fan out into the three mountain chains that traverse Colombia, stretches a vast territory covering hundreds of square miles, where some of the nation's most impressive archaeological remains have been found. Among these are big stone statues of fierce, jaguar-fanged men. These are often double figures eight to fifteen feet high, which guard mesitas and tombs with massive stone sarcophagi. The rocky bed of one river in the area has been carved into a series of interconnected channels and pools. The clear water flows over decorative figures of snakes and frogs, and there is one crowned human figure.

San Agustín itself, and the neighboring village of San Jose de Isnos, at 5,600 feet above sea level, are situated in a well-watered, fertile, temperate valley close to cooler, productive uplands and warmer lowlands. A large variety of fruits and vegetables and a double crop of maize are available to the inhabitants during the year.

The valley lies at the junction of easy communication routes: east to west from the Pacific coast to the Amazon, and south to north from Peru to the valleys of the Cauca and Magdalena rivers, which until they join before flowing into the Caribbean Sea, divide the Andes to the north.

Tierradentro ("the Inside Land") is some seventy-five miles north of San Agustín in more broken country. It has similar stone statues. In addition are found many rock-cut, painted tombs with columns and niches that are reached by stairs carved in the soft sandstone.

It is known that these attractive environments were occupied by the sixth century B.C., and that successive waves of new peoples lived there at least until 1400 A.D. Around that date the area seems to have been abandoned. The numerous wooden-framed houses rotted away, vegetation covered the rubbish heaps with their thousands of broken pots and tools, and the region reverted to dense forest. Warring forest tribes lived there from that time.

Most of the gold objects from San Agustín are small, and they are scarce. They consist of pendants, nosepieces, earrings, and beads for necklaces. Some pieces are hammered and others cast. Unused or leftover gold buttons and wire indicate that these people were goldsmiths and that the pieces are not trade goods derived from another zone.

From Inza, in Tierradentro, comes one golden masterpiece, a hammered jaguar mask with curvilinear decoration at the top and sides. The fangs, like the tusks of the stone statues, seem to have been designed to strike awe and terror into the hearts of those who beheld them.

There are some stylistic resemblances between late San Agustín and the Calima zone, particularly in the details of the heads of statues and those of gold pins, in pottery, and in the feline motif.

SINU

Near the Caribbean Sea the Cauca river swings east to join the Magdalena, with which it has flowed parallel for most of its course. West of the Cauca, and bounded by the last foothills of the Andes, the coast, and the Gulf of Darien, there lies a relatively flat region from which are derived the Sinú style gold pieces. The San Jorge and Sinú rivers divide the area, and there are numerous lagoons with abundant and varied bird life. Reptiles and fish are plentiful. Maize formed the basis of the inhabitants' diet, replacing manioc at about 500 B.C.

Important burials took place in huge mounds which were easily located and thus soon looted by the Spaniards. Grave goods included many fine gold pieces.

Nosepieces and earrings of incredible delicacy and precision were cast in one piece by the lost wax process, which means that a wax model had first to be made in a hot tropical climate, and every tiny duct formed in the clay mold had to receive its share of the molten metal. Modern jewelers are at a loss to explain how such perfection could be attained.

Birds of the region are represented in heavy goldwork. The eagle, spoonbill, and egret can be identified. Reptiles appear as finials on the heads of ceremonial staffs,

and the widespread jaguar motif is present in a small jaguar with a spiral motif, and in a fine large piece of a seated animal with similar decoration on its back. There are flying fish or butterflies, and figures, some double, of animals which seem to have existed only in the imagination of the artist. Others, such as a twin deer staff head, are very realistic representations.

TAIRONA

On the foothills of the Sierra Nevada de Santa Marta and in the surrounding plains on the landward side expert goldworkers lived. The name of one tribe, Tairona, is used for this archaeological zone.

These people had an advanced social organization and were beginning to use stone in their architecture and engineering. The Tairona were maize farmers, but their land also yielded a varied diet of fruits and vegetables from several climatic zones. The number of net sinkers found shows that they also exploited maritime and riverine resources.

The Tairona's interest in stone extended to symbolic or decorative objects. They made axes, staffs, and wing-like objects which hung from their elbows to tinkle when dancing. They manufactured vast quantities of tubular beads in quartz and carnelian to combine with gold pieces in beautiful necklaces.

Tairona goldsmiths produced small lightweight figures of gold, seemingly because they had little gold in their area. Most pieces are made of gold-copper alloys and were gilded by oxidation. The frog seems to have held special significance for them. Hundreds of tiny specimens have been found, most of which take the same form. Fierce, naked figures, wearing huge curvilinear headdresses, and jewels in the nose, ear, and lip, are characteristic of the Tairona zone. These figurines, which are pendants, are perfectly finished. Earrings were lacy, crescent-shaped objects, formed in two or three planes. Several styles of nosepieces and plugs in the lower lip were worn. The golden lip plugs are varied in form, and usually come in two parts, a curved piece to rest against the teeth, and a decorative piece that fits over the first through a slit below the lower lip.

Flat plates, worked in low relief, depict scenes of daily life. Almost all of the plates from this zone were found in huge burial urns.

The Tairona is the only group described in this essay whose descendants still live in the same area. Now, without their gold, they have retreated to the high, remote valleys that lie within the vastness of the Sierra Nevada de Santa Marta.

TOLIMA

The name "Tolima" is given to a gold style that comes mainly from the upper Magdalena basin. Here the valley carved out of the Andes is wide, flat, and very hot. We know little of the peoples who inhabited this area in pre-Hispanic times, except that they buried their dead in painted urns and produced a distinctive style of goldware.

Large, flat, stylized figures, with geometrically disposed arms and legs, and long, anchor-like tails characterize this area (Figure 4). Stylized bats are also common.

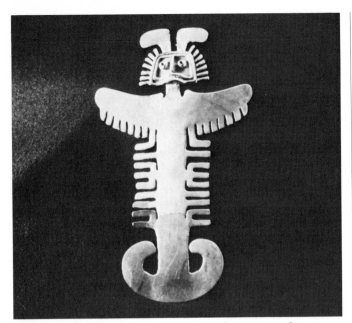

Figure 4. *Pendant representing anthropomorphic figure.*

Figure 5. *Geometric pendant, the "Guaca del Dragon."*

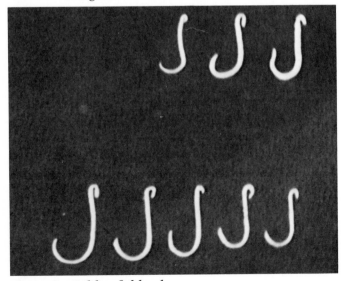

Figure 6. *Golden fishhooks.*

One masterpiece, though found outside the zone, belongs to this style. This is the "Guaca del Dragon," illustrated here and whose likeness is on the poster designed for this exhibition (Figure 5). Only the semicircular face is modeled. A diadem of delicately cut gold surrounds a visage with "coffee-bean" eyes on spiral decoration, a long, straight nose from the forehead to the rectangular mouth showing all its teeth. The rest is almost abstract, a play of right angles with holes and lines echoing the linear decoration of the diadem around the face above.

NATIVE USES OF COLOMBIAN GOLD

The pre-Hispanic gold objects had a variety of uses. Judging from the evidence of the seventy tribes that survive today in Colombia, the objects and their decorations also must have been rich in symbolism. Regrettably, this symbolic aspect was never studied. Now, thanks to the essay of G. Reichel-Dolmatoff in this catalog, new insights into that symbolism have added significant dimensions to the objects.

An important use of gold was for personal adornment. In some tribes, such as the Tairona of the Sierra Nevada de Santa Marta on the Caribbean coast, men, women, and children used gold or jewels to beautify themselves. The tribesmen habitually wore nose rings, plugs in the lower lip, earrings, breast plates, crowns, bracelets, anklets, finger rings, and necklaces. All were made either of gold, often mixed with other alloys, or were mingled with quartz or carnelian.

Gold and ceramic figures surviving today illustrate how the Indians used these pieces. And chroniclers left their own impressions of these people:...naked, but adorned with splendid golden jewels. Cieza de León, in his Chronicles of Peru, says:

"When they went to war they wore crowns, large medals on their chests, and beautiful feathers and bracelets, and many other jewels...I remember seeing Indians covered with gold from head to foot."

Gold was used in architecture. Another chronicler, Fray Pedro Simón, tells about this use:

"Outside of the doors of the houses were hung fine gold plates called 'chaguales,' that were the size of a platter, more or less, and were hung to catch the reflection of the rays of the rising and setting sun. They were also hung in order to hear the sound that they made, although rather deafening, as they clanged together, when the two large doors were opened and closed."

And still another contemporary account by Father Pedro Simón describes how the Indians used gold in sculpture in the region of northeastern Colombia:

"They [the Spaniards] entered a house that was on the corner of the plaza, a house so large that it could easily hold 2,000 men. In the house they immediately found twenty-four idols, or wooden busts, like great giants, all gold-plated from head to foot. The figures were facing each other, half of them in the form of men, and the other half in the form of women. Each of them had a mitre or tiara of the finest gold carved on the head, and hung from one shoulder to the other ham-

mock into which they threw the gold that the Indians offered them in that sanctuary."

Such statues and offerings were quickly melted down and sent to Spain.

The natives had many gold objects for their personal use. These included spoons and cups of gold, and, according to the stories of the famous conquistador Mariscal Jorge Robledo: "...(men of importance) drink with gold cups that weigh 300 *castellanos*...they have spoons and vessels of gold." Women combed their hair with gold combs, but few of these survive. One extraordinarily beautiful example in the Museo del Oro, Bogotá, seems to represent a sheaf of grain.

Poporos, receptacles for the lime used in the process of coca-chewing, were also for personal use. But since coca was of religious significance, we will consider these objects later.

Many other objects in the current exhibition were used as a mark of personal prestige or to designate the function of their owner. Staff-heads, or finials, from the Sinú region designated the status of their owners.

Gold was employed extensively in daily work. Many gold and copper needles were made, each with different designs on the needle eye, depending on the work for which it was used. Fishhooks were also made of gold (Figure 6).

Two types of metal tools are known (Figures 7–9). Some are large, in the form of a half-moon, or like large modern-day chisels and are made of copper. Others are delicate and resemble present-day dentists' tools. They are so tiny that it seems they could only have been used for making the wax models of the objects fabricated by the lost wax process.

It is doubtful that these Indians used gold as money, but gold did have a value in barter. There is no gold in the Muisca area, yet the Muiscas had many gold objects. They obtained the raw material from tribes living along the shores of the gold-bearing rivers in exchange for salt, cotton robes, and emeralds.

The religious uses of gold were numerous and important. In the Muisca region gold was commonly used as an offering. Tiny gold figures, naked, and replete with such details as weapons and necklaces, were votive offerings that were thrown into sacred lakes, or were put into ceramic vessels for burial with the dead.

The entire ceremony of El Dorado revolved around the use of gold as an offering. In the sacred lake of Guatavita, the chief, covered with gold dust, immersed himself in the water. The gold fell to the bottom of the lake, and at the same time his subjects threw offerings of gold and emeralds into the lake. The golden offerings were shaped in various forms: men, women, children in cradles, chiefs in their houses, warriors with trophy heads, hammocks, birds, seashells, pots, alligators, lizards, snakes, *poporos*, trays, *butacos* (seats), litters, and large baskets. One extraordinary object depicted a human sacrifice where the victim was tied to a tall post and shot at with arrows, his blood symbolizing rain.

An extremely important use of gold was to make objects which were buried with the dead. Variations

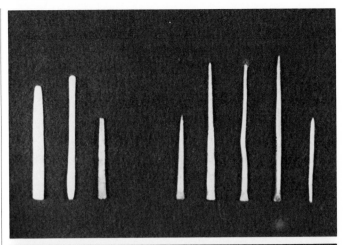

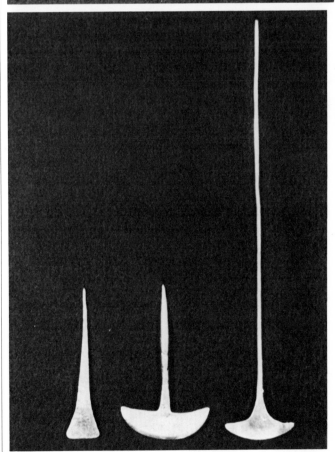

Figures 7–9. *Tools, uses unknown, but perhaps for working gold or performing surgery (e.g., trepanning).*

among cultures are great. The differential treatment in the burials within a single area indicates distinct social classes.

In the Muisca zone of the Sabana de Bogotá, around the present capital of Colombia, the burials were simple. Bodies were covered with thin, flat stones and the offering was often limited to a single piece of low-quality gold. There also were secondary burials in urns.

In the Calima region urns assume a simple but beautiful form and at times contain bones painted with annato (a red dye) and a single piece of gold. But the majority of the gold pieces that were funerary offerings come from the sunken tombs. Such tombs consist of a type of well, ranging from three to forty-five feet in depth, with one or more lateral chambers excavated to one side, at the bottom. It is possible that this funeral custom originated in Middle America.

Colombian tombs vary greatly in form and range from simple niches at the foot of a shallow shaft, to elaborate, painted chambers with several spaces, situated at the base of rock-cut staircases. These elaborate forms are found in Tierradentro, near San Agustín. Most of the Museo del Oro's collection comes from tombs of this type in various regions of Colombia.

In life also, gold was frequently used for religious rites. Evidence from existing tribes in Colombia indicates that the Indians used hallucinogenic drugs as an integral part of their complicated religious and philosophical systems. On important occasions, the men of a tribe might take *yagé, yopo,* coca, tobacco, *chicha,* and other drugs. The priest-shaman, or tribal cult leader, recited the tribal myths and explained the hallucinations, thus assuring the unity of the group and reinforcing its moral principles.

Coca is a shrub whose leaves, when chewed with an alkali such as lime, produce the stimulant cocaine. The Kogi, a contemporary tribe that inhabits the Sierra Nevada de Santa Marta, say that coca clears the mind, and that they use it daily during discussions. The *poporo* is the vessel in which lime is carried.

An Indian puts some coca leaves in his mouth. He then wets the small stick, or spatula, with saliva, puts it in the poporo, so drawing lime out on the wetted stick. Modern poporos are made from a gourd or calabash, but in the past some were made of gold.

Lime was obtained by burning and grinding seashells. It is a curious fact that in the Sabana de Bogotá, in Muisca territory, 375 miles from the coast there are many seashells which the Muiscas obtained through barter. They were considered sacred, and many gold figures represent them.

We know from the chroniclers that the Indians also used other drugs. Juan de Castellanos wrote in 1582 about tobacco and Jimson weed *(Datura* spp.). Describing the sacrificial burials at Tunja he says:

"...in order that neither the woman nor the slaves feel miserable upon their death, the Xeques give them, without their knowing, certain drinks of tobacco essence and other leaves of the tree that we call borrachero (Datura)..."

We have information about a snuff called *yopo* prepared from the toasted and pulverized seed of *Anadenanthera peregrina,* from Pedro Buillén de Arce, a parish priest among the Tunebo in 1634. He gave this description of a feast of the natives:

"...that night with their rites and ceremonies, crushed yopo was taken from a shell covered with a 'lion's' tail, and divided with some spoons of 'lion' grueso (bone) by an old man. Thus it was until sunrise and then, in the morning, the cacique had prepared the female Indians with much food and drink that they breakfasted and such Indians were not allowed with their spouses that night."

In the Museo del Oro there are many gold *yopo* trays. The majority carry two pairs of animals as ornamentation. This symbol is repeated in the statues of San Agustín.

Despite the fact that so much of the great treasure of pre-Columbian America was destroyed, or seized to be melted down to fill the coffers of Europe as bullion, miraculously, it seems, a small part of it has survived. The world's finest collection, or more than 29,000 gold pieces, is maintained by the Museo del Oro in Bogotá. Of the more than six hundred pieces loaned for this exhibit, some five hundred are theirs. They are depicted in this catalog larger than life so that you may examine them in detail and wonder at their fresh originality and, in many cases, both their intricacy and artistry.

Things of Beauty Replete with Meaning— Metals and Crystals in Colombian Indian Cosmology

by G. REICHEL-DOLMATOFF

Introduction

The treasures of El Dorado are among the most haunting images our age has inherited from the colonial past.

Gold and emeralds, pagan rituals, temples and shrines watched over by sun priests and warriors, are all part of the Indians' highly developed lost civilization about which we know too little because of the ruthlessness and greed of their conquerors, which we still find unforgivable. Historians and anthropologists have rightly denounced the appalling inhumanity of the Spanish Conquest, and have described in detail the political, economic, and moral causes and consequences of the looting of the lands of El Dorado.

However, they have done this from a European point of view, and few of their works face the deeper significance of the destruction of the cultural values of an entire civilization, which was an accompaniment of Western colonial expansion. Aboriginal cultures based upon millenniums of intellectual efforts were broken up in a matter of a few years. The endeavors of millions of people to make sense out of existence and to make life meaningful were annihilated as crude superstitions. The destruction was so complete that there are extensive regions in America with almost no information about their inhabitants in the sixteenth or seventeenth centuries. Nothing is known of their languages, their social organization, or their religion. Most tribal societies simply disappeared, became scattered, or were completely modified soon after their first contacts with the European invaders. Of many tribes of the tropical lowlands or the cordilleras of Colombia we only know the names, preserved in lists of tributaries or of forcible converts to the Christian faith.

And only in a few cases did chroniclers take the time to describe what they were able to learn about native customs. The greed for gold had become the main incentive for the conquest of El Dorado, and occasionally the chroniclers would describe some aspects of an aboriginal society when referring to tribes exceptionally rich in gold. Those who were not, hardly deserved their notice. But the Muisca of the Bogotá highlands, the chiefdoms of the Cauca Valley, and some tribes of the Caribbean coast, all of whom were proficient goldsmiths, did attract the Spaniards' attention, and in this manner the earliest chroniclers have left us some descriptions of their ways of life. But the meaning of the gold and the reasons for its form were not mentioned.

Europe had a rich lore referring to the symbolic meanings of metals and gem stones, their supposed relationships to astronomy, and their magical influences upon their owner's health and fortunes. No information has survived on what the Indians thought of *their* treasures. At best we have anecdotes. Precious stones were offered to the sun; emeralds were burned in sacred fires. But there is little else in the chroniclers' writings to identify what the Indians themselves thought of metals and their alloys, of their specific uses and properties, of mining and of the processes of metallurgy. The entire symbolic context is lacking, for the gold appeared to Western eyes only as an economic asset. Even the Aztec jewels that had been sent to Charles V and which Albrecht Dürer admired so much on his journey to the Netherlands, were melted down soon after.

Many studies have been made of the amount of gold brought back to Spain; of mining and taxation, of hoards melted down or struck into coins to pay for new wars and new quests for more and more riches. And many historical studies have been published on the tremendous impact this new source of wealth made upon European economy and society. But all these studies of how and why these golden treasures and gem stones were valued so highly by the conquistadors and their lords are written from the point of view of the assayer of carats and the chronicler of the divine rights of kings. The historians discussed the Indians' use of gold but they referred to it only as a European index of wealth, as idolatrous offerings to false gods, but hardly ever as things of beauty replete with meaning. Nobody seemed to have asked the Indians themselves what it was they saw in their gold, what it meant to them in their world of primitive trade relations devoid of a monetary system.

When archaeology came of age in the lands of El Dorado, specialists began to discuss the technology and aesthetics of pre-Columbian gold. Metallurgical studies analyzed the different alloys and described *tumbaga*, the compound of gold and copper which many Indian tribes used for their adornments. Typologies were established and stylistic analyses were propounded, sometimes for the purpose of tracing far-flung trade relationships. Iconographical studies were considerably rarer, and many of them contained dubious interpretations. A knowledge of aboriginal religions and mythologies was needed to approach this field; in fact, what was needed for an approximate understanding of iconographic elements was a thorough familiarity with local ethnography and linguistics. But few archaeologists or metallurgists had this background, and so many iconographic studies exist based upon very personal interpretations that bear hardly any relationships to ethnographic facts.

A severely limiting element was the circumstance that most objects of gold, gilded copper, or other metals were completely lacking in associations. They had been found by treasure hunters, ignorant peasants who destroyed the evidence contained in the stratigraphy, the pottery, skeletons, domestic architecture or burial furniture, and who, often enough, when selling their spoils, would lie about their exact provenience. It is a sad fact that only very few objects of Colombian gold have been found by archaeologists in controlled excavations. For this reason, practically all publications on the gold and emeralds of El Dorado are based on museum or private collections in which the artifacts and gem stones are seen out of context. Many of these publications are picture books or catalogs. The accompanying texts quote weights and measures, mention some metallurgical and technological details and perfunctorily restate the same time-worn ideas that have already been expressed in previous publications. They duly quote Fray Bernardino de Sahagún on technology, Albrecht Dürer on aesthetics, and Sir Walter Raleigh on the *Golden Citie*, but in the end they leave the reader with the stale sensation of *déjà lu*, only occasionally relieved by some splendid photographs of what the respective author called an "alligator deity," or some other designation of his fancy.

The value of gold, then as now, depends upon its purity, and the value of an emerald depends both upon its flawless deeply green color and its size. It was this standard that counted at the European courts, and in the coffers of the merchant princes and church dignitaries. It was the brilliance, the weight, the purity and the sheer quantity that counted. Only these qualities would buy power and luxury, and could be stored away as an investment for the future. Exactly as today, almost half a millennium later.

But gold and gems are only symbols. A nugget and an uncut emerald have a price only insofar as a symbolic value is attached to them, and has been agreed upon by people. And symbolic values are relative. They can vary widely from one group of people to another, or from one age to another. We know (or believe we know) why we value the treasures of El Dorado. But what do we know of the value attributed to them by their legitimate owners, the Indians? What was the symbolism of gold and copper, of emeralds and rock crystals among the Indians of Colombia, at the time when the Spanish invaders arrived? It is obvious that these objects meant something entirely different to the natives, and that this difference, at first, appeared incomprehensible to the Indians. But then, at some stage of our analysis, there will come an instant when we begin to wonder about this difference in attitude and meaning. At times there will come a sudden flash of recognition, of comprehension of a pattern of thoughts which seem to link shamanistic concepts to the deeper levels of our own cultural tradition.

What comes to mind when looking at the bewildering variety of prehistoric metal artifacts are questions of meaning. The ancient goldsmiths depicted an enormous range of objects: men, animals, plants, miniature artifacts, entire scenes of people in action. Or they fashioned flasks, bowls, and spoons, masks for the dead or drinking cups for the living. Some objects are strictly geometrical or represent life forms in stern abstraction. Others are naturalistic, while still others flourish into baroque exuberance.

But there are some recurrent themes that cut across cultural boundaries and chronological phases. There is the hieratic personage carrying a staff; the heraldic woman sitting with spread legs; the masked man with a huge headdress and a horizontal bar in his hands. This scroll-bearer, as one might call this image, appears in many guises, carrying a bifid or double-scrolled object similar to a crosier, or to some tendril-like botanical form. And one might mention many other themes. The question still remains: what do these objects illustrate?

Some of the characters are chiefs, we might suppose. Others could be ancestors and mythological beings. Some are forces of Nature, even gods. There may be totemic animals, or monsters seen in visions and dreams. But what about the abstractions, icons whose meanings escape us altogether? Perhaps in the future some symbolic associations can be established by painstaking research based on excavations, typology, and stylistical analysis, but the significance of many of these objects will be forgotten forever.

Another approach to the problem of meaning does exist, however. In Colombia several tribes still survive which traditionally use metal ornaments of aboriginal manufacture. The Desana and other Tukanoan Indians of the Northwest Amazon have necklaces and pendants of metal, and the Chibcha-speaking Kogi and Cuna Indians of northern Colombia still use heirlooms of gold and copper alloys, although they do not manufacture them anymore. The Chocó Indians of the Pacific Lowlands manufacture personal ornaments of silver. Among all these tribes the significance of gold, silver, and copper jewels can still be observed in its traditional context, and the artifacts are made and used according to the traditional meanings the shamanistic world view has attached to them. It is surprising, then, that this complex of technological knowledge and esoteric concepts has remained neglected by anthropologists for so long, because it contains a large body of relevant information, not only for our appreciation of prehistoric metallurgy, but also of the workings of the shamanistic mind in general. It is this dimension, then, I shall attempt to explore in the pages that follow.

I shall try to reconstruct some of the fundamental ideas the Indians had about metals and crystals, in the context of their particular world views. In doing so I shall take recourse to ethnographic analogies, to the early Spanish chroniclers, and to archaeology. I am the first to admit that some of my suggestions are highly hypothetical, but even so, I believe that they might provide an interesting glimpse into the world of aboriginal symbolism and metaphor, and make us forget for a while our modern world's preoccupation with the price of ounces troy and the new gold rush.

In my survey I shall refer to three native cultures of Colombia: the present-day Tukanoan tribes—mainly

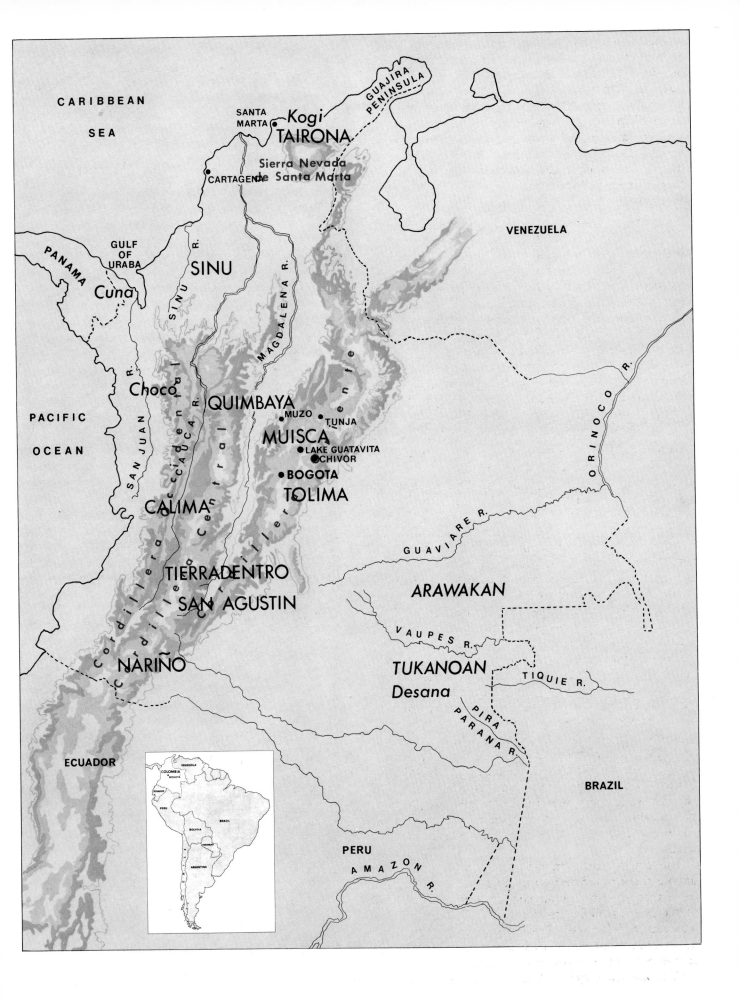

CARIBBEAN

SEA

SANTA
MARTA

Kogi
TAIRONA

GUAJIRA
PENINSULA

Sierra Nevada
de Santa Marta

VENEZUELA

CARTAGENA

GULF
OF
URABA

PANAMA

Cuna

SINU

SINU R.

MAGDALENA R.

ORINOCO R.

PACIFIC

OCEAN

Choco

SAN JUAN R.

QUIMBAYA

MUZO   TUNJA

MUISCA

LAKE GUATAVITA
CHIVOR

BOGOTA

TOLIMA

CALIMA

Cordillera Occidental

Cordillera Central

Cordillera Oriente

CAUCA R.

ORINOCO R.

GUAVIARE R.

TIERRADENTRO

SAN AGUSTIN

ARAWAKAN

VAUPES R.

Cordillera Oriental

NARIÑO

TUKANOAN

Desana

TIQUIE R.

PIRA PARANA R.

ECUADOR

BRAZIL

PERU

AMAZON R.

19

the Desana—of the equatorial rain forest of the Vaupés territory in the Northwest Amazon; the Kogi Indians of the Sierra Nevada de Santa Marta on the Caribbean coast; and the Muisca Indians, who were the ancient inhabitants of the highlands of the Eastern Cordillera, in whose heartland the Spaniards discovered the sacred lake of Guatavita, and founded the capital city of Santa Fé de Bogotá. It was at Lake Guatavita where the ritual of El Dorado, the Gilded Man, was celebrated in ancient times.

Desana Metallurgy and Symbolism

To most readers the image of Amazonian Indians is that of naked painted savages wearing colorful feather-crowns, and hunting monkeys and crocodiles. Adventure films, sensationalist journalism, and popular travel and missionary reports have contributed to create this utterly misleading stereotype of one of the world's most interesting regions. Thus, it may be difficult to connect rain forest conditions with golden jewels, and to realize that many Amazonian Indians of today are the deculturated remnants of once-powerful tribes that half a millennium ago enjoyed a much higher level of development than that of their modern, semi-"civilized" and missionized descendants.[1]

Let us first examine the role of native metallurgy among the Tukanoan tribes and their immediate neighbors. A characteristic personal adornment consists of small triangular plaques of hammered and polished silver which are strung together to form a necklace (Plate 1). From early travel reports it appears that these ornaments were common until fairly recent times.[2] Some that are in use today are heirlooms and are said to have been handed down for generations. But others are of recent manufacture and have been made by their present owners by hammering a silver coin into the desired shape. The manufacture of these simple but decorative objects presents no technological problems, and the quality of workmanship is fairly uniform from one region to another. Individual necklaces may vary in size and number of triangles, and tasteful combinations with black or red beads made of perforated seeds or with animal teeth may enhance the value of a particular specimen.

Another metal adornment consists of ear-pendants which are worn by the men on certain ritual occasions. They are shaped like short tubes that have been split in half, and are usually made of hammered copper. People say that in former times they were made of gold. At present they have almost disappeared, but I have seen some that had been made by cutting a brass shotgun shell in half.

The fact that these traditional ornaments still exist among these rain forest tribes, and that they are still being made, offers an unique opportunity to learn more about their symbolic importance. The following tale was recorded from the Desana Indians and provides some information on the tradition of metallurgy in the rain forests of the Northwest Amazon.

"The one who taught us to make copper ear-pendants

PLATE 1. A shaman of the Barasana tribe wearing a necklace of silver triangles and animal teeth, and a polished quartz cylinder. Pira-paraná, Vaupés territory, Northwest Amazon.

was a fugitive. That was in the days of the Creation. He was a stranger; he was not a fugitive, but he was like one. He was a master in these things. He had some molds of yellow clay. Nearby there was some yellow water. There, without anyone being allowed to watch him, he took water and put it into the mold. In this way he made many ear-pendants. They were of two metals: white and yellow. The material was extracted from a pit, like a mine. That pit was lost.

"He was not of any tribe of ours; he was called nyahpa mahsë, 'copper person.' The yellow material is like fine grains. This man also taught us to make some little animals, butterflies of silver. He taught us how to make molds.

"When the Spaniards came there was an end to it. But it is known where his things are hidden. They say that in that place there is a spirit-being which appears all of a sudden. He is called Copper Person; he is tall and red-faced. His eyes are like fire. He wears these long ear-pendants which shine like fire. He is good; no one is afraid of him."

This story contains a number of interesting details. First, it would seem that metallurgy was not autochthonous, but that it was introduced from the outside, at least among the Desana. Second, the description mentions a form of mining, the casting in molds, and the use of "two metals: white and yellow." The rest of the tale contains some mythical embellishments, such as the motifs of the mysterious stranger and his prohibition to watch him at work; the motif of the lost mine and the hidden treasure, and lastly, the stranger's appearance as a "tall man, red-faced," with glowing eyes, a standard way of describing certain forest spirits.

Although all this information is highly condensed, the few descriptive details acquire importance as soon as we look at them within the context of Tukanoan culture. The origin of the stranger is perhaps of minor interest. He may have come from the Andes or from the Guiana Highlands. But the "two metals" call for attention. The text says that the metals were "white and yellow," and one is tempted to think of silver and gold, but this is not the case. We have discussed this text with a number of Indian informants and have learned that what is designated here as "white and yellow" does not refer to actual metallic colors, but to abstract qualities, to an invisible "white" creative force, and to a visible and material yellow potential. The commentators explained that these two forces met and mingled in different proportions. The basic material state was the visible sun, associated with gold and with human semen, while the "whiteness" was a modifying abstract cosmic force which heightened or diminished the quality of the golden component. Further discussion led to the problems of fertility, solar energy (as understood by the Indians) and, above all, human fertility and the rules of exogamy. In Tukanoan color symbolism white and yellow are associated with male potency, a brilliant white standing for solar energy, while yellow represents male potency and the creative forces contained in human semen, the pollen of certain plants, in the heat of a fire, or in the flash of a drug-induced vision. Yellow is symbolically the most important color for the Desana, who distinguish some thirty different hues, intensities, and values that range from a pale yellowish to a deep orange color.[3]

Complementary to this male color symbolism of white/yellow, we find a color range of reddish hues. Red is said to be a female color because of a number of particular associations. In the first place, red is the color of blood, and blood is, according to Desana theories of conception, a basic component of a new life; conception takes place when yellow semen and red uterine blood fuse in the womb. This fusion, however, occurs only if the child is conceived under culturally favorable conditions, that is, both parents must be ritually pure, and prepared for the event. The blood of the mother must be "living" blood, as the Indians call it, not blood that has begun to turn into menstrual blood. In the second place, red is the color of heat, of fire, of transformation. The process of intrauterine embryonic development is imagined as one of "cooking," of the embryo being transformed in a fiery furnace, a crucible. The color combination yellow/red stands, therefore, for male/female fertility and fecundity.

In Tukanoan mythology and cosmology the sun represents a male-fertilizing principle associated with the yellow color range, while the moon is female. Her colors are variable because they depend entirely upon the influence of the sun; they range from yellow-green to a dark red-orange and to blue-violet, depending upon *"how the sun makes her change."* Both Sun and Moon are imagined as human prototypes, as a heavenly couple that exemplifies male/female relationships, be they between husband and wife, father and daughter, or brother and sister. The normal husband/wife relationship is seen in the monthly relation between Sun and Moon; the apparently intertwining paths of the two are seen as an ideal process of fertilization, conception (First Quarter), terminal pregnancy (Full Moon), and birth (New Moon). In fact, the Indians say that the waning moon is copper-colored. This color association, however, is valid only when the moon is referred to as an anthropomorphic female; if referred to as a principle of plant growth the associated color would be green.

In Tukanoan shamanistic thought we thus have several parallel images. The relative motions of sun and moon are equated to male/female relationships, to embryonic development, and to the metallurgical process by which different metals are being alloyed. This last parallel needs further explanation. All Tukanoan tribes, some twenty or more, are grouped into phratries each of which consists of three intermarrying tribes the members of which speak their own language. Exogamic laws are very strict. Compatibility between marriage partners is partly described as a form of compatibility of "toxic" qualities which are said to be inherent in a man's semen and in female blood. To this are added a number of other criteria, such as odor and flavor, qualities which are partly based upon pheromonal[4] considerations, are highly abstract and can be ascertained only by shamans. Any marriage union becomes a matter of balancing what the Desana call "color energies" with their corresponding "odors" and "flavors." Mythology and shamanistic lore abound in descriptions of the compatibility or incompatibility of spouses, and this problem of combinations is of great concern to shamans and elders.

The metallurgical parallel refers precisely to this complex of ideas. Ideally, the sun fertilizes a brilliant New Moon which, at reaching First Quarter, proves to be pregnant. Moon then passes through a sequence of yellowish, reddish, and copper-colored phases which are compared to the menstrual cycle and to the process of embryonic development. At the same time, this process is said to be a model of metallurgical combinations.

The Spanish chroniclers, as well as later travellers and missionaries, tell us that among a number of Indian tribes, both on the Caribbean Islands and on the mainland, copper objects were more highly valued than gold. The reason for this seems to have been the peculiar odor one can perceive when rubbing copper or *tumbaga* objects between one's fingers, a smell many Indians find, if not downright attractive, at least highly significant. We have seen that in our Desana tale, copper was called *nyahpá*. I have discussed this term at great length with my informants who explained its meaning in the following manner. The term *nyahpá* (or *nya'pá*) is said to be related to the verb *nyaári*, "to transform." The copper ear-pendants are called *nyahpá mahí*, literally, "copper-bars," or "transformation-bars." The word "bar" refers here to a stick or a rod-like shape. Now in

Desana symbolism the ear-pendants represent testicles or, in a wider sense, male potency. Many myths and tales tell of a young man's quest for these objects which are jealously guarded by his elders. Occasionally these "elders" will be identified with the sun or with a thunder being; in any case, with a father image. To "receive the ear-pendants," "to lose them," or "to recover them," are recurrent myth motifs.

On the other hand, a certain frog is known by the name of *nya'pá* and the Indians pointed out that its name was related to the above-mentioned concepts, that is to say, to copper, ear-pendants, sex, and the concept of transformation. The form itself was said to symbolize the female sex organ, a comparison which is common among these and other tribes.

The informants said: *"The frog is nayaari-pa, meaning 'transformation-vessel' or 'transformation-receptacle,'"* and went on to explain that it was "a means of transformation," of procreation. To this was added that this particular frog had a protective coloring—a trait which proved its "cunning" and that its body had a "sucking," absorbing quality which made it difficult to detach the animal from whatever surface it held on to. The most important characteristic of the frog, however, was said to be its peculiar odor *(sëríri)* which was said to be identical to copper.[5] The associations are thus the following, as summarized by the native informants: copper ear-pendants have a phallic tubular shape or are compared to testicles; their polished brilliance signifies virility, and their odor relates them to sex and to a certain frog with female connotations. It turned out that this complex of associated ideas was well-known to many people.

This leaves us with the triangular pendants made of hammered silver which I mentioned at the outset. The Desana call them *pogóru*, "butterfly," and this again is a fertility term which is derived from *poréri*, "to burst open, to dehisce, to scatter pollen or semen"; *goru*, "efflorescence."[6] In this case, however, the symbolism is not expressed through color, but refers to the triangular outline of the object. Among the Tukanoans the triangle is an important concept of abstract relationships. I have mentioned that a phratry consists of three exogamous tribes that constitute a triadic relationship of exchange patterns. The population of each tribe consists of patrilocal males and virilocal females; in other words, an abstract phratric territory is imagined as a hexagon and, indeed, the entire Vaupés territory is thought to constitute one huge hexagon encompassed by six major waterfalls.[7] The Tukanoans thus distinguish between "male" triangles, pointing upward, and "female" (pubic) triangles, pointing downward. In shamanistic imagery the superposition of these triangles represents coitus; the two triangles meet and slightly overlap at their meeting points, and this junction becomes a point of life-giving transformation.

Let us look, then, from a shamanic point of view, at a necklace made of silver triangles. Since each triangular plaque is suspended from its pointed apex, they all are said to be male symbols. The point of suspension is an

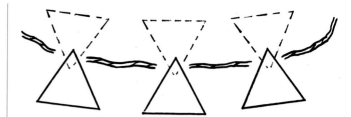

FIGURE 1. *Schematic view of silver triangles and their symbolic projections. Tukanoan Indians, Vaupés territory, Northwest Amazon.*

articulation, a contact with an invisible, abstract female triangle which is located above the visible male pendant (Figure 1). In a shaman's view, therefore, a necklace consists of a series of hourglass-shaped elements which symbolize a male/female union and thus express a concept of fertility and transformation.

During the dry season, when the water level of the rivers is low, one often can see large numbers of white, yellow, or red butterflies flying upriver. These swarms form undulating masses that sway in fluttering waves which move both in a vertical and a horizontal sense. The sight of these long-stretched chains of butterflies has a very specific meaning to the Indians. In the first place, the color associations are white, yellow, and red and refer, as we have learned already, to fertility concepts. The insect flights during the wet season complement the fish runs to the spawning beds upriver during the wet season. Second, the chains of butterflies are compared to necklaces, the Nature's *pogóru* necklaces. The vertical and horizontal wave pattern of the insects' flight is compared to the alternating visible and invisible silver triangles of a necklace, and shamans add that these swarms of butterflies are a common hallucinatory experience during narcotic trance states in which fertility symbolism is prominent. The word for necklace means, literally, "bursting efflorescence." This image of invisible symmetrical mirror images—like the opposed triangles—is common in shamanic thinking, and can be applied to many other phenomena, such as a house, a hill, a person, a basket, or a hearth. Everything has an invisible complement and thus expresses the fundamental principles of dualism, reciprocal relationships, and procreation.

Although the Tukanoan rain forest tribes have only these two simple metal artifacts—the ear-pendants and the triangular butterflies—we are fortunate that these objects continue to be in use, because their complex symbolism offers an insight into what some aspects of metallurgy and metal artifacts may have meant to prehistoric tribes. We must accept the possibility that precious metals and jewelry had an entirely different meaning to the aborigines, than they had—and still have—to Western civilization. From the attitudes and ideas formulated by the present-day Tukanoan tribes we may deduce the following: the main importance of personal metal adornments lies in their symbolic associations expressed in their alloys, coloring, shape, and odor. All these traits are closely related to concepts of insemination, pregnancy, and fertility. Possession of these objects carries with it a certain prestige, but their true importance does not reside in their commercial, material value, but in their fertility associations which the owner and his society can establish whenever the object is being displayed. It is worth mentioning here that among the Tukanoan Indians the concept of "adorning oneself" always has the meaning of decorating the body with sexual symbols, with signs of virility, or of female receptiveness. Feather-crowns, the white down feathers of the Harpy eagle, body paint, aromatic herbs, ritual artifacts such as staffs or adzes, they all carry quite explicit sexual meanings, and the symbolism of shiny metals thus forms part of an all-important pattern of courtship and mating behavior.

The Desana distinguish between two categories of ritual adornments. One is associated with chiefs, warriors, and servants, and consists of carved staffs, clubs, stick rattles and certain adzes, feather-crowns, and seminal symbols such as white down feathers. This category is called *mohó*, literally, "weapon, armor," and symbolizes procreation and male dominance. The second category is associated with shamans, dancers and singers, thus with ritual specialists who are mediators between opposing forces, between the sexes, or between complementary social groups. This category is called *buyá* and consists of shiny bead or teeth necklaces, metal objects, or tinklers. The literal translation of *buyá* would be "adornment," but the term rather means "energy" *(bogá)*, as seen to be operating in the form of sensorial stimulations by colors, shapes, sounds, smells and movements.

To put a carved staff and a glistening tinkling necklace into the same category of so-called ritual objects does not make any sense to an Indian who interprets the former as an insignia of male assertiveness in a world of aggressive action, and the latter as an enticing and seductive object meant to induce the wearer and the beholder into a dream-like dimension of sensorial experiences. Both categories are, therefore, vehicles for the communication of specific meanings which, as I have mentioned before, reach far beyond the sphere of mere display and wealth. Adornments, then, are interpreted first of all as sensorial stimulants. Their brilliance, colors, and jingling sounds are said to produce specific states of mind, and their use during rituals in which hallucinogenic drugs are being consumed, is said to be essential in triggering and modifying the colorful visions of the participants.[8]

Desana Shaman's Crystals

I shall now discuss crystals, which have a marked symbolic value among the rain forest Indians of the Vaupes territory.

Rock crystals of different sizes, most of them just a few centimeters in length and of varying degrees of transparency, are important shamanic power objects. Although they do occur in many local geological formations, good quality crystals come mainly from the regions lying to the north of the Vaupes, which are occupied by the Arawakan tribes of the Isana, Inirida and Guainia rivers. Rock crystals have many characteristics that call the attention of shamans. First, their hexagonal structure constitutes an important model, an ordering principle, which repeats and perpetuates itself as a kind of "memory" of nature. Hexagonal shapes and spaces are all-important in shamanic thought. They can be found in honeycombs, wasps' nests, in the horny plates on the carapace of certain land tortoises,[9] in spider webs, and in certain constellations of stars.[10] The recurrent hexagonal pattern provides an image of order and continuity referring, above all, to shamanistic concepts of primordial energy, the powers of transformation, and the principle of seminal fertility. Phratric territories are conceived as hexagonal spaces, and hexagons are structural features of domestic architecture and of certain other material artifacts. A second characteristic is the following: under certain light conditions, especially in the flickering light of an open fire, one can observe, in the depths of a fairly translucent crystal, a cluster of colorful reflections. Indeed, when slowly turning a crystal in one's hand one can perceive the entire color spectrum. I have mentioned already the native concept of "color energies." The Desana and their neighbors believe that the "whiteness" of solar energy contains the color range of "male" yellowish and "female" reddish hues, accompanied by the range lying between yellow-green and red-violet, and which expresses a range of energies related to growth, ripeness, putrefaction, decay and death. In shamanic thinking, the sun is a huge rock crystal, and every rock crystal on earth is a miniature sun, thus containing all these vital energies. In one shamanic image, solar energy is contained in human semen, and a rock crystal consists of condensed, concentrated semen. In fact, rock crystals are called *ëhtabohóru*, a term that can be glossed as "transformer-condensed-male object."[11]

Apart from these readily observable characteristics— the hexagonal structure and the color spectrum—shamans seem to have observed other, more complex properties. In fact, some seem to know about piezoelectricity and the effect opposite charges on different crystal faces can have upon dust particles. Occasionally Tukanoan shamans speak of very special crystals that have differently colored zones or bands arranged in a sequence across the crystals' longitudinal axis, an observation which most probably refers to tourmaline, a mineral which occurs in neighboring Brazil and might easily have been traded over large distances. Tourmaline has the property of attracting or repelling ashes or dust, a quality that shamans have observed in rock crystals and which they relate to criteria of compatibility or incompatibility of marriage partners. If a phratry is a hexagon, then each pair of adjoining prism faces would correspond to a "male" and a "female" component which, in the shaman's view, would then correspond to a concept of opposition, of attraction and repulsion, or of prescribed and forbidden marriage partners. In Desana terms, a positive charge *(bogá)* is female and attracts, while a negative charge is male and emits energy *(tulári)*. An additional property of tourmaline is that it acts as a polarizer and that by looking through it, one can locate the position of the sun, even if the sky is covered with clouds.[12]

Shamanic crystals are used for many different purposes. A shaman might imagine himself to be enclosed in a huge crystal, and to be looking out of it as if watching a radar screen. As a diagnostic tool, a crystal might be slowly passed over the body of a patient, while watching for subtle changes in reflections and transparency. Tiny amounts of finely-pulverized rock crystal can be used as an invigorating medicine. However, crystals are never used for scrying, for fortune-telling, or for locating lost objects.[13] But there are many other uses and a good-sized translucent rock crystal is a shaman's most treasured possession.

A characteristic adornment of Tukanoan shamans consists of a polished quartz cylinder which is suspended from the neck (Plate 1). The whitish quartz comes mainly from some outcrops on the Tiquié river where the Indians are specialists in the manufacture of these objects, first by rough chipping, and then by polishing them with fine quartz sand. The hole is drilled with a hardwood stick which is twirled between the hands while another person provides quartz sand as an abrasive. The finished artifact is about 12 or 15 centimeters long. Since the manufacture of these quartz cylinders is a lengthy process, and the raw material is not readily available, these ornaments are valuable possessions, but their true importance resides, once more, in their symbolic associations. A shamanic quartz cylinder is called *abé yeru*, "sun-penis," and like the rock crystal, is imagined to consist of solidified semen. Shamans and headmen wear these ornaments to demonstrate their magical generative powers.[14]

Gold Among the Tairona and Kogi Indians

Let us examine now some aboriginal beliefs about semi-precious metals and minerals in an entirely different region of Colombia. The Kogi Indians, a Chibcha-speaking tribe of the mountain valleys of the Sierra Nevada de Santa Marta in northern Colombia, are among the few surviving native groups whose social, political, and religious institutions still contain elements which are characteristic of the ranked societies of the ancient chiefdoms of northwestern South America. It was among these chiefdoms and incipient states that metallurgy became highly developed, and a knowledge of present-day chiefdom-derived cultures is of special importance for the study of the symbolism of this particular branch of art and technology.

The Kogi are the modern descendants of the Tairona, one of the major chiefdoms which in the early sixteenth century had reached a level of incipient statehood characterized by large urban centers, a powerful priesthood, and an efficient economic basis of intensive maize farming.[15] The Spaniards had established contact with the Tairona already in the late fifteenth century and it was in Tairona territory where the basic patterns of future conquest were established by the invaders. To them, the Indians were idolatrous pagans, savages sunk in ignorance and brutishness. It took the Spaniards the better part of a century to subdue the Tairona. The last great rebellion occurred in 1599 and was suppressed in 1600 when Spanish troops burned and sacked the villages, executed all chieftains, shamans, and their relatives, except those who had been able to escape into the mountains. The Kogi, numbering at present about 6,000, are the last survivors of this great defeat.

At present, the Kogi constitute a scattered peasant population, but lordly and priestly lineages with a strong sense of privilege and rank still exist, plus a fairly elaborate political administration. As a matter of fact, Kogi religion, philosophy, and historical traditions are of a complexity which can be compared only with that of the advanced cultures of Mesoamerica or the Central Andes.[16]

PLATE 2. *Ancient Tairona jewels as used by present-day Kogi priests. San Miguel Valley, Sierra Nevada de Santa Marta.*

This stands in strong contrast to the extreme simplicity of present-day Kogi economy and technology. The fields are poor, the houses are bare and contain only the most elementary furnishings. All artifacts of daily use are coarse and almost completely devoid of ornamentation. Kogi life appears on the surface to be very drab. This impression, however, is misleading. In reality, the Kogi lead a very rich inner life and partake fully in their elaborate and colorful cultural tradition. Moreover, what is truly striking is the Kogis' fascination with a past rich in gold and all kinds of semiprecious stones. In their flight into the mountains and over the centuries of persecutions by encroaching peasants and missionaries, the Indians have been able to save some Tairona pieces of gold, gilded copper, and polished stones, and on rare ceremonial occasions Kogi priests will wear these ornaments, before hiding them again in secret mountain caves (Plate 2). The Kogi will talk for hours and for whole nights about the gold of their ancestors, the "sacred gold," as they call it, and will recite and sing of golden masks and crowns, of bracelets and necklaces, ear-pendants and wristlets, of untold treasures that were taken from them, or are hidden away in inaccessible places. To hear a Kogi priest speak of these things which are half-fantasy, half-historical reality, evokes a sense of tragedy that spans the centuries. In these tales, as in no other native tradition, the voice of the vanquished becomes a powerful indictment of the greed, the ignorance, and the injustice which our modern world still shares with the darkest sides of the Spanish conquest.

The Kogi are a deeply religious people. Their belief system is based upon the teachings of a great Mother Goddess, an all-embracing being who is the beginning and the end of all individual existence. This mother image is also very exacting, and demands the strictest discipline from her children. Apart from the observation of a moral code which is a guide to everyday life by insisting upon collaboration, reciprocity, honesty, and an utterly non-materialistic attitude toward existence, the Mother Goddess demands obedience to a number of very strict laws of order, of regularity, and balance. People are expected to lead a frugal life; nothing should be done in excess and everything should be predictable. The life of man as an individual and as a social being must be completely geared to the cosmic clockwork of orbits and cycles; to the motions of the sun, moon, and stars; to seasons, to all recurrent phenomena that can be observed and predicted in the skies and on earth. Man must be like the sun, or like a constellation. Woman must be like the moon, waxing and waning. Both must grow and ripen like plants, like maize plants.

This emphasis on order, together with the fear of dissonance, are ever-present in Kogi thought and lie at the basis of most religious concepts about the structure and functioning of the universe. However, the Kogi are well aware of the fact that the cosmic order is not as perfect as it appears to be. They have observed phenomena, such as eclipses. They know the irregular path of the moon, and the wandering motions of Venus and other planets.

According to sacred tradition, it was the Mother Goddess who, after having created the earth, appointed sun and moon as divine time-keepers and guardians of the cosmic order. The Great Mother Goddess had five sons who were the Lords of the World Quarters, the oldest son, called Mulkuéhe, being Lord of the Center and having the attributes of a Jaguar God. The ground-plan of this earth was a quincunx, a square with a sacred central point, a model that is endlessly repeated in Kogi cosmogony, cosmology, geography, the siting of villages or ceremonial centers, the construction of temples, the framework of looms; or in mental images of social and religious relationships.[17] Once the earth had been created with the help of the Five Lords, the great Mother appointed Mulkuéhe to become the sun. The name of this Lord contains the root, mul, which refers to brilliance and "whiteness," in the same sense as it was among the Amazonian Indians. Mulkuéhe wears a golden mask and his chest is covered with a huge golden disk. The many versions of the Creation Myth describe how this god and Jaguar Lord first married a golden

toad called sëlda bauku, who betrayed her divine husband and was rejected by him. Ever since, toads are the sun's enemies and call together clouds and rain to obscure his brilliant face. Next, Sun married Rattle Snake, called Takbi, but this marriage also failed because of her violent character. At last, Mulkuéhe married Moon, called Namsháya, a jaguar being. Their daughter was Venus, called Enduksáma.

In one version of the myth, Sintána, the second-born son of the Mother Goddess, but in many ways the most important one, serves as her messenger and went in search of a place on earth called mulkódakve, where two children (siblings?) were said to live. Sintána found the place and asked the boy: "Do you want to be the father of the earth?" The boy replied that he did. He then asked the girl: "Do you want to be the mother of the earth?" And she too agreed. He now dressed the children all in gold, and when he had done so they rose into the air and appeared in the sky as Sun and Moon. Their first child was Venus, a girl.

By appointing this nuclear family as "parents" of the earth and of mankind, the Mother Goddess meant to establish an ever-present model for human behavior and above all, for the morality of family life. As in many aboriginal cultures in Colombia, celestial bodies and phenomena are taken to be models and mirror images of what is happening on earth, and all dissonances in the heavens, such as eclipses, shooting stars, comets, or the unusual proximity between two celestial bodies, mirror dissonances on earth. This means that the earthly problems of adultery and incest are equally present in the sky, and Kogi interest in astronomy is partly determined by the scrutiny of astral motions in search of indications of similar social disturbances on earth. In fact, Sun commits adultery with a number of constellations, and eventually commits incest with his daughter Venus, being misled by her double image as Morning and Evening star.

The Kogi personification of the sun is a jaguar, and moon is represented as a mountain lion. In some versions Moon is Sun's sister, and she too is a jaguar. In any case, there is a close relationship between Moon and the jaguar, which is exteriorized by the fact that both are spotted. In a number of myths the origin of these spots is explained as a stain, a macula that the Moon Feline acquired in punishment for incest with her brother, the Sun Feline. It is well-known that jaguar imagery in the American tropics is closely related to fertility concepts.[18] The jaguar sun god is thus a very ambivalent being, part progenitor and creator, part aggressive devourer. The Kogi see in this ambivalence the image of Man, of the individual torn between matter and spirit, and the essence of Kogi religion refers to the need for finding a balance between the conditions necessary to physical survival—food, sex, and dominance—and the equally necessary satisfaction of spiritual and psychological needs. Both are based upon the concept of fertility, the seminal illumination which guarantees not only social continuity, but leads to a process of individuation and intellectual achievement. And it is gold which symbolizes this seminal light.

Among the Kogi, just as among the Desana, gold and other metals are not valued as economic assets, and not as indices of prestige-carrying personal wealth, but as a symbolic fertility potential that belongs to all of society. In fact, the Kogi say that it belongs to mankind at large, and that its life-giving energy is not limited to their culture alone. This idea identifies once again the golden substance with solar energy.

At certain times of the year, Kogi priests will collect a number of ritual ornaments of gold and gilded copper, place them upon a special mat and then expose them to the full rays of the sun. This act is supposed to charge the objects with a fertilizing cosmic energy that will be transmitted to the priests and, through them, to all participants in rituals involving these ancient objects. On certain ceremonial occasions related to solstices and equinoxes, Kogi priests will wear beautifully carved wooden masks topped with elaborate feather-crowns. Many of these masks are centuries old, and some of them are clearly Tairona heirlooms, corresponding stylistically in every detail to archaeological objects of gold, pottery, or stone. Sometimes the sun is represented by a jaguar mask, at other times by a mask representing a quite realistic human face.[19]

The huge fangs of certain jaguar masks are occasionally encased in golden sheaths and are worn in combination with necklaces and bracelets made of cotton ribbons or cords to which Tairona gold or copper adornments have been attached. These objects may be bird effigies, strings of little frogs or lizards, small bells and other tinklers, combined with bar-shaped bead-strand spreaders adorned with wire scrolls (Plate 3).[20] The ceremonial dress worn by priests with a certain sun mask called *surlí*, consists, among other parts, of a skirt-like apron to which a phallus of cotton cords is attached. White cotton threads and fluffy unspun cotton always have a seminal connotation, quite similar to that of the white down feathers of the Harpy eagle, among the Tukanoan Indians.

Many sun masks exist because the sun is personified by a diversity of mythical and divine beings. The main personification is Mulkuéhe, but sometimes his brother Sintána appears as a sun god. Another solar personage is Téiku, called the "Lord of Metals and Metallurgy." Although mainly associated with gold and gilding, in modern times Téiku is being designated as the Lord of Axes and Bushknives, and people who wish to obtain and safely use these tools must make the corresponding offerings to him. At certain ceremonial centers Téiku is honored with solemn dances and songs. Another solar being is Nyíueldue, "sun-gold-elder brother," who is Téiku's son-in-law and is also called the "Father of Gold." Another is Duginávi, "brother-jaguar," a heroic gold-related sun being, sometimes associated with Orion.

The solar divine most often mentioned as being in charge of gold is Téiku, and it is interesting to analyze his name. Téiku is related to *téishua*, a fertility word that is used in a wide range of meanings that refer to

PLATE 3. A Kogi woman wearing a necklace of ancient Tairona beads of semi-precious stones. Hukumeishi, Sierra Nevada de Santa Marta.

"old, ancient, primordial, legitimate male descendant," etc. The word *teisháua* means "testicles," but can also be used to refer to any substance by which a creative, transformative process is set in motion. The word *téi* designates a cultivated field; a rattle is called *tái*, and in many native cultures of Colombia these instruments have phallic connotations. The hardwood tree guaiacum *(lignum vitae)* is called *táishi* and has similar associations. This brings us to a tentative interpretation of the ancient tribal name Tairona, pronounced *teiyúna* or *teishúna*, by the modern Kogi. According to the Indians, Tairona means "the true males, the male ancestors, the progenitors." The association between gold, the sun, and the principle of fertility becomes thus fully confirmed.

Crystals and Other Minerals in Tairona-Kogi Beliefs

Turning now to the role of minerals and crystals in Kogi culture, an entirely new dimension opens before our eyes. The Sierra Nevada de Santa Marta is very rich in colorful minerals, especially in quartzes of many different kinds. Translucent rock crystals, carnelians, agates with beautiful veinings, chalcedonies, and many others are found in river-beds and outcrops. There are no emeralds in the Sierra Nevada, but the Spaniards obtained some from the sixteenth-century Tairona who had gotten them by trade with the provinces of the Andean interior. The Tairona had finely-carved figurines of dark greenish nephrite, another material which is not autochthonous, but which is evidence for the Indians' interest in rare and beautiful minerals, especially of a green color.

The Tairona were specialists in making enormous amounts of finely polished necklace beads of many different materials, shapes, colors, sizes, and surface textures. There is hardly an archaeological site in the area that would not have yielded a large amount of tubular, globular, or barrel-shaped beads. From many archaeological finds it would seem that these colorful beads were not used exclusively for necklaces, bracelets, or pendants, but that they had ritual significance. One of the first Spanish chroniclers who wrote on the Tairona, says: *"On that day they obtained a piece of cloth of six or seven varas in length and half that wide, with many interwoven designs, and among them many stones: carnelian, dark green agate, and jasper"* (Oviedo, VI:137–138).

In many house or burial sites of the Tairona, loose stone beads have been found in carefully-covered pottery vessels or in special caches constructed with a set of dressed stone slabs. Other caches of multicolored beads have been found in association with the typical circular house foundations, near one of the two entrances, under the doorsteps, or at the foot of the principal houseposts. At Cerro Azul on the Sevilla river, the floor of a circular structure was found to consist of a meter-thick layer of accumulated earth which contained thousands of beads in all stages of manufacture, ranging from large pieces of raw material, to roughly chipped forms, half perforated beads and, finally, the finished products. Some of these beads were oversized roughly-shaped blanks or bits of stone, some thirty centimeters in length, while others were finished beads that were up to twelve centimeters long and very heavy. None of these could have been worn as personal adornments, and it is clear that they formed the floor of this probably-ritual structure because of their symbolic significance. Near Nahuanje, 8,000 beads were found in one single burial (Mason, 1936: 212), and 5,000 were found in a jar beyond the Don Diego river. Alden Mason's field catalog mentions the following quantities:

large tubular (beads)	36
small tubular	750
large discoid	13
small discoid	2100
Total	2899

Among the present-day Kogi these ancient Tairona beads are greatly esteemed. All Kogi priests own a number of carefully-selected and matched specimens, and most women wear several strings of necklace beads, in which precious archaeological specimens are combined with modern trade beads of glass or porcelain, or with safety pins and shirt buttons of plastic material (Plate 3). Many of the archaeological beads the Kogi possess are heirlooms. Others were acquired from lowland peasants or treasure hunters who find prehistoric Tairona sites and sell the beads to the Indians. Indeed, the trade in Tairona necklace beads seems to go back for centuries before the Spanish conquest, and to have covered a very extensive region, far beyond the Sierra Nevada. Spherical carnelian beads are greatly valued among the modern Guajiro Indians, where they often form part of a high-ranking woman's bride price, and modern jewellers in the large cities sell Tairona bead necklaces for high prices.

According to ancient European traditions many precious and semi-precious stones were thought to cure or prevent diseases, and to bring luck or, conversely, disgrace to their owners. The Spaniards were impressed by the sheer mass and ritual importance of the beads they saw among the Tairona. The chronicler Juan de Castellanos, who in the mid-sixteenth century lived for some time in Tairona territory, writes: *"They perforate blood-colored stones, not bad for diseases of the kidneys"* (1850:322). Another chronicler writes: *"...they work and perforate stones of many virtues, that are found among them, such as (to cure) blood, colic, milk, urine, and others..."* (Simon, 1882:IV:356).

This use of semi-precious stones was quite unfamiliar to the Indians who had very different ideas about the importance of these minerals. Tentatively we can reconstruct some of their beliefs, based on the use the present-day Kogi make of these ancient stone beads. I have mentioned the Tairona habitation sites caches containing large numbers of beads. Among the Kogi, the following custom is still being practiced: Every time that a new house or a new temple is consecrated by a native priest, a number of necklace beads are put into a small clay vessel which then is buried in the center of the floor, or near the main entrance. In the case of a domestic structure, the number of beads corresponds to the number of adults who will occupy the house. When a temple is being consecrated, the beads correspond to the members of all initiated men's families. Perforated beads indicate female household members, while unperforated beads stand for males, or occasionally for uninitiated adolescent boys. The important point, however, is that each person, male or female, is through lineage associated with certain minerals and certain colors. His or her lineage considers itself to be the magical owner of this material. In addition, each mineral, color, shape and texture, corresponds to a certain phenomenon of nature, to a plant, an animal, an illness, a cardinal direction, or to a certain mythological or divine personification. All categories that constitute this universe have their specific "owners, fathers, or mothers," and these personifications call for offerings which in many cases consist precisely of these necklace beads, or at least small fragments of them. Such offerings represent food for the ancestors and divine bearings, but since food is equated with sex, just as is the case with the rain forest tribes, the beads acquire a seminal connotation, and the offering is equivalent to an act of fertilization, with the explicit purpose of increasing the fertility of the respective "owner" or parent of a certain category of vital substances. For example, in order to protect and increase a certain food plant, its magical owners must be fed and fertilized with a mineral substance that corresponds to that particular food plant.

Kogi priests distinguish between some fifty or more different types of beads *(kuítsi)*, some of which may belong to a particular person or lineage, or may be given to him or her under certain circumstances. Some of these beads represent permanent permission to carry out an activity or occupation, for instance, marriage, coca chewing, or maize planting. Others prevent or cure diseases, or protect their owners against aggressions and accidents. Many are used as offerings. A tiny fragment is broken off and is ground to a fine powder, which then is wrapped into a thin maize leaf. The act of offering consists in opening the small bundle and of blowing the powder away, or in scattering it over a certain spot. Only high-ranking priests will make offerings in which whole archaeological necklace beads are pulverized.

The most important mineral is the rock crystal. It is called *nyi kuítsi*, "water-stone bead," and is believed to consist of a seminal substance. Necklaces of tubular beads of highly polished or frosted rock crystal are treasured heirlooms, but many priests own natural crystals of various sizes that have not been modified.

Rock crystals are especially associated with the priestly lineage whose name is *kurcha*. The *kurcha* are designated as "Owners and Keepers of the Rock Crystal," and as "Owners of Water" or "Owners of the Seed." Apart from this they are associated with the Right Side, the North, the concept of "whiteness," and the cane from which pan-pipes are made. Their particular necklace beads *(súnyi)* are of translucent quartz and have an elongated tubular shape. Others of their beads, called *kurcha kuítsi*, are of whitish quartz, with fine red veins, and are small and of tubular shape. The *kurcha* are the high priests who trace their origin back for many centuries before the Spanish conquest. The continuity and legitimacy of this lineage is of great concern to the Kogi, and its origins and extraordinary achievements are celebrated in myths, songs, and genealogical recitals.

The name *kurcha* has important meanings and associations. The term (sometimes pronounced *kulcha*) means "seed, sperm, origin," and in a related symbolism, refers to "pupil of the eye," and to "vision." The sexual symbolism of the eye and of visions (in the sense of a supernatural act of impregnation through the eye) is often mentioned by Kogi and Desana shamans. In the ancient Tairona language which survives in some sacred songs, the word *kutsha* means "rain," another fertility symbol, while *kuncháua* means "eye" and *kunchálula* refers to "egg, semen, seed, fruit." It is to this cluster of ideas that the Kogi refer when they say *"the kurcha are our seed."* According to myth, the original progenitor of the *kurcha* lineage was called *kuncha vitabuéya*, literally, "seed-half span long," an expression that was glossed as "penis" by Kogi commentators. The mythical mother of the first *kurcha* was called *kulcháha*.

The animal the *kurcha* identify themselves with is the opossum, called *maktu*, in Kogi. There are several reasons why this fairly common creature should be an important ancestral being. In the first place, the bifurcate penis of all didelphidae suggests potency, and the Kogi say that if a man eats opossum meat, his wife will bear twins. The short gestation period (twelve to thirteen days), and large litter size (average of seven) also suggest great fertility. The opossum's nocturnal habits make it, of course, a shamanic animal. But the truly important characteristic is that the local race of opossum common in the Sierra Nevada de Santa Marta has six digits instead of the usual five. Now there is a great deal of consanguinity among the *kurcha*, and polydactylism is said to be fairly frequent. It is not considered to be an abnormality, but a sign of legitimacy. Thus, a child born to *kurcha* parents, with six fingers or toes, was surely lawfully begotten.

Indeed, the number six has a very specific significance to the Kogi. The word for six is *téishua*, and immediately we recognize its relationship with the cluster of fertility words I have mentioned earlier. In fact, *téishua* not only means "male ancestor," but means "ancient, seminal, primordial," and is also used to designate the original Tairona language. What, then, is the connection with the number six? Just like the Tukanoan Indians of the Northwest Amazon, the Kogi believe that the hexagonal structure of rock crystals represents a cosmic ordering principle, the crystal itself being a seminal substance. Archaeological specimens of natural crystals have been found in many Tairona burials,[21] and similar crystals are still in use as offerings in increase rituals. The seminal quality of these crystals is alluded to in myths and tales and the number six has a truly sacred character.

In Kogi astronomy an image prevails that is similar to one the Desana have elaborated. Six large and brilliant stars, centered upon Orion, form a celestial hexagon which then is projected upon the earth. The entire Sierra Nevada is conceived of as a huge rock crystal encompassed by sacred sites and divided by radiating rivers into six regions which are the spacial models for social and ritual organization. The same hexagonal model underlies the siting of ceremonial centers, and constitutes the groundplan of all temples. In shamanic images of the afterworld, the dead ascend the steep slopes of the Sierra and, when reaching its top, enter into the icy prism of the snowpeaks. Six, then, is a sacred number; it is found in social organization and in the framework of a loom; in architectural units or in patterns of ritual behavior. In the word *téishua* the Kogi combine the ideas of the hexagonal ordering principle and the principle of fertility, into a great synthesis of Man and the Cosmos.

It is interesting to observe more general Kogi attitudes toward crystals, gemstones, and minerals. The concepts of "being translucent like a crystal," of "turning into stone," or of having "a heart like a precious stone" are shamanic idioms and images which are frequently mentioned in myth, ritual, and esoteric conversation. The whole Sierra Nevada is seen as a petrified world in which each individual mountain is a temple, the snowpeaks are gleaming white crystals, mountain lakes are prism surfaces, and most any huge boulder is an ancestral being. Strange rock formations, erratic blocks, slabs or columnar shapes, caves and crevices all are surrounded by innumerable myths and tales referring to the stone parentage of the ancestors. There are petrified temples, petrified treasure chests, petrified ships, petrified animals, a ghostly world of landmarks among which the present-day Kogi move about as if it were an immense museum in which their entire cultural tradition is on display as a permanent guide for the living. While wandering over the mountains and valleys of the Sierra, a Kogi has only to read the many messages his senses perceive in order to live according to traditional norms. The sense of formality, of rigid ritual behavior, and of an all-pervading discipline is expressed in this image of a petrified environment. At the same time this mineral world, peopled by hundreds of "monuments" to the past, and animated by their mute but persistent voices, provides a deep sense of security. A Kogi always feels this watchful presence of the great assembly of ancestral beings, and knows that he is a living link in this chain of traditions.

Muisca Gold and Precious Crystals

The Chibcha, or Muisca as they called themselves, are the third aboriginal group to which I shall refer. The Muisca occupied the mountainous districts of the Eastern Cordillera, especially the fertile highland basins of Bogotá and Tunja, in the provinces of Cundinamarca and Boyacá. Muisca culture, like that of the Tairona, had developed beyond the level of a tribal society and, by the early sixteenth century, was beginning to show the characteristics of an incipient, but already well-organized state. Tribal traditions and the Muisca language disappeared in the eighteenth century.

The Spaniards discovered hoards of gold in many sacred sites of the Muisca, and extorted still more from chieftains, priests, and the population at large. Flat anthropomorphic figurines of elongated triangular shape and highly stylized features, most of them about ten centimeters in length, are very distinctive of Muisca gold work. Other gold objects consist of diminutive representations of common artifacts, and small groups or scenes in which people are shown in different attitudes, in houses, on rafts, or encumbered with ritual or domestic objects. From archaeological research and from early written sources we know that most of Muisca gold or *tumbaga* objects were used as offerings. Like the Tukanoans and the Kogi, the Muisca professed a solar religion in which the energizing powers of the sun were exalted, and gold or other shiny metals became the earthly representatives of these life-giving forces of the cosmos. Many offerings of gold or gilded objects were made at mountain lakes, on hill tops, or at sacred caves or boulders dedicated to some divine being. Other golden artifacts were used as personal adornments and insignia, and have been found in burials.

In many cases the fertility associations of these gold offerings are obvious. For example, certain pot-bellied female effigy vessels of clay were found to be filled with small golden figures, probably representing the great Mother Goddess Bachué who with her offspring peopled the world. Golden offerings often were wrapped into wads of cotton, or were combined with small effigies made of white cotton thread, a material which among the Chibchan tribes of the Sierra Nevada has a seminal connotation.[22] These figurines of cotton were sometimes adorned with emeralds and thus constituted a common way of presenting an offering.[23]

Other fertility associations might be seen in the sacrificial use the Muisca made of powdered gold. In fact, El Dorado, the Gilded Man, was the protagonist of the Muisca ritual at Lake Guatavita, which fired the imagination of generations. According to tradition the chieftain covered his naked body with a thick layer of gold dust adhering to a resin base, and then submerged himself in the center of the lake, washing off the gold and throwing into the depths still more offerings of golden jewels and emeralds. This dramatic scene, showing the chief on his ceremonial raft surrounded by attendants, is represented in an elaborate artifact which is among the most prized possessions of the Gold Museum in Bogotá.

The Muisca had two mineral resources, the possession of which enormously enhanced the competency of their trade relations. These were salt and emeralds. The brine from the large salt mines located at several highland sites was boiled in big pottery vessels, and the heavy cakes of salt were traded over vast regions, far beyond the limits of Muisca territory. The boiling of the brine, it is interesting to note, was a female occupation, but trade itself was a male enterprise. In view of the symbolic value which many surviving tribal societies attribute to salt, the importance of the Muisca salt trade probably went beyond that of a mere exchange of commodities, and may have constituted a system of reciprocal symbolic loans aimed at maintaining a balance of political and religious influences.[24]

Emeralds, on the other hand, carried a fertility symbolism which is made clear in an ancient Muisca myth recorded by a Spanish chronicler. The myth tells that, according to a shamanic vaticination, the daughter of the chieftain of Guachetá was to become the carnal bride of the Sun God. Every day the maid exposed her body at dawn to the first rays of the sun until she became impregnated by the divine force. After nine months, to the consternation of everybody, she gave birth to a huge emerald. The girl wrapped it in white cotton, but then the stone burst open and from it emerged an infant which grew up to become the great chief Goranchacha. He was designated as a legitimate Son of the Sun and, in later life, built a sun temple near Tunja.[25]

Emeralds have a hexagonal structure, the same as rock crystals and tourmaline, and in this recurrent phenomenon we can trace a consistent pattern of shamanistic thought which unites the Muisca with the Tukanoan tribes in the south, and the Chibchan tribes of the Sierra Nevada in the far north of the country. Large rock crystals have been found in priestly burials of the Muisca and emeralds were considered by them to be sacred stones to be used as offerings to the gods. The Muisca traded their emeralds as far as the Caribbean coast.

It seems that the peculiarity of a common hexagonal structure was an element of great significance to the Indians, more important by far than other characteristics of the three crystals in question. It is interesting to observe that many of the emeralds that were taken from the Muisca by the Spaniards, were found to be of very poor quality by modern standards. It would seem that flawlessness, a deep green color, and a large size were not especially appreciated by the Indians, to whom the hexagon and an undifferentiated greenish hue were more significant than the exacting criteria of modern gemologists and jewelers. The same can be said about the quality of gold used in offerings or personal adornments. In many cases the objects contained a high percentage of copper, or were made of gilded copper, and so had little or no value to the Spanish assayers. It seems that the Indians thought differently and sometimes attributed a high value to objects made of alloys.[26]

Symbolic Trade

There are no gold-bearing deposits in Muisca territory, and thus the raw material for their goldsmiths had to be obtained by trade with neighboring tribes who did have access to such mineral sources. Copper deposits, however, were frequent among the Muisca and the Indians manufactured many objects from *tumbaga*, that is, from alloys or almost pure copper.

Muisca trade relationships, like those of most other tribes of prehistoric and early colonial Colombia, consisted of far-flung networks comprising specific overland routes, institutionalized markets or trade posts, and particular forms of contacts between different cultural areas. Often enough there existed trade relationships between groups that otherwise professed to be enemies. Since no monetary system was in existence, all trade was based upon the exchange of goods, either local raw materials or manufactured or processed objects.

The principal trade items in early Colombia consisted of gold and copper, emeralds and semi-precious stones, necklace beads, cotton (raw fibers, plus spun and woven goods), salt crystals or cakes, sea shells, and some other products, such as dried fish and narcotic snuff. This list can be reconstructed readily from archaeological and historical sources and at first view seems to contain only items which might be traded by peoples in many regions and countries (Plates 4 and 5).

However, if we take a closer look at the individual trade items and their pattern of exchange, we can observe certain peculiarities. First of all, emeralds, gold, necklaces, exotic shells, condiments, and finely woven cloth are luxury goods, at least to our minds and, most probably, to the Indians' as well. But when examined with the eyes of the ethnographer and ethnohistorian acquainted with the shamanistic ideology of the modern descendants of the very same tribes whose ancient trade we are studying, it becomes obvious that all these trade items have a marked symbolic value which refers to concepts of fertility and fecundity. We have discussed already the different fertility associations of gold, silver, copper, hexagonal crystals, necklace beads and white cotton thread, and so we can turn now to some other trade items which appear in the list quoted above.

Salt and mollusk shells have strong fertility associations in the ideology and trade relationships of several present-day tribes of Colombia. In shamanic ideology of the Tukanoan tribes of the Northwest Amazon, the Chibchan tribes of the Sierra Nevada, the Chocó Indians

PLATE 4. *A Noanamá Indian wearing ornaments of hammered silver. Chocó territory, Docordó.*

of the Pacific lowlands, and many other native groups, salt symbolizes sex. It is semen, or it is said to be an aphrodisiac condiment.[27] Shamans and their apprentices are not allowed to consume salt, and any person preparing himself for a ritual event should abstain from the use of salt. Among the Kogi, a certain dance in which, exceptionally, women participate quite actively, constitutes the central event of a yearly salt ritual during which different categories of salt crystals are being called upon in songs and spells. The ritual lasts for several days and ends with the solemn distribution of certain small sea shells which symbolically represent the female sex, and constitute talismans whose possession authorizes their owners to consume salt.

A shamanic distinction is made between rock-salt crystals and sea-salt crystals. Traditionally, the so-called "green salt" was obtained from the beaches occupied by the Guajiro Indians lying to the northeast, while "white salt" from the ancient *Matuna* tribe was gathered from the beaches of Dursino and Papare, near the modern city of Santa Marta. In any case, all salt acquired by the Kogi had to come from outside their territory, and their exchange trade offering was the transparent rock-salt of their mountain habitat. It is understood that this salt trade symbolized the exogamous exchange of women, together with a balancing of abstract energies contained in the salty substances.[28]

Salt symbolically is related to lime, the fine white powder that many Indian tribes obtain by ritually burning small sea shells, or the shells of land snails, which

PLATE 5. *A woman of the Cuna tribe wearing an ancient nose ring of gold, and a silver breast ornament of recent manufacture. Arquía, Gulf of Urabá.*

they then consume together with chewed coca leaves.[29] Sea shells or the shells of land snails of different shapes, sizes and colors are important in Kogi and Tukano shamanism, where they represent male and female principles. Penis covers made of large sea shells (or of gold, imitating a shell) have been found in various archaeological contexts. Among the Muisca of the sixteenth century, marine shells, large and small, formed part of practically all offerings at ritual sites or in private shrines. Sometimes small pieces of gold were introduced into these shells which then were wrapped into cotton, a triple association of fertility concepts.[30]

The El Dorado Illusion

In the preceding pages I have described a body of modern and ancient aboriginal beliefs and attitudes toward certain precious metals and crystals which were found by the Spaniards among the Colombian Indians of the sixteenth century. From ethnological, archaeological, and historical sources it is possible to reconstruct a train of thought by the light of which we can appreciate some of these objects and artifacts within the wider context of shamanistic ideology and everyday aboriginal life.

It is clear that many of the symbolic values the Indians attached to gold and gemstones were similar to those held in other epochs in the Old World. From ancient times through the Middle Ages, to the Renaissance and beyond, people tended to see energizing and fertilizing forces in gold and gems, and have attempted to master and use their supposedly hidden powers for their personal ends. Alchemy, Astrology, and Black and White Magic all were concerned with the energetic principles men claimed to see in metals and minerals. Within this context the discovery of the lands of El Dorado was a wondrous encounter with an already darkly glimpsed magical dimension of metals and stones concealed in the matrix of a great Earth Mother, the dimension of mineral embryology, the *Petra Genitrix* of hexagonal shape, and the mystery of transformation in the crucible.[31]

But in their final appreciation, gold and gemstones occupy a place on the natives' scale of values which differs widely from Western thought. This difference lies mainly in the small regard the Indians had for purity in gold and flawlessness in emeralds. What to us seems to be of utmost importance in determining the value of the object seemed to have been of little concern to the Indians. Our view of the valuable essence of the material was not theirs. They treasured some other aspect they saw in it, such as its particular mineral structure, its dull luster, or even its peculiar odor. True, many splendid archaeological pieces survive which combine the highest achievements in technology and artistry, but which are made of gilded copper or *tumbaga*, which we, disparagingly, would call a "base" metal. Nor would weightiness and solidity seem to have been desirable features. Many gold or *tumbaga* Colombian artifacts look slightly tinsel-like, having been made from thin sheets of metal, cut in straight lines. Obviously the flat smooth surfaces were meant to reflect a tropical sky, or the lights of fires or torches, in dark sanctuaries. The objects were meant to shine, to throw back the light of a brilliant sun, not to glow with the inner fire we would associate with a precious jewel. And other gold artifacts consist of spindly wires, of lattice work and filigree, techniques which yet enhance this lack of weight and volume.

Emeralds were never cut or polished, and so are devoid of the brilliance we admire in modern gems. Many ancient emeralds that have been found in shrines or burials are greenish lusterless stones, and it is clear that the Indians' standards of an emerald's worth were not the same as ours.

In summary, gold and emeralds had meanings and values we do not share with the Indians. To them they were divine generative forces, cosmic forces which guaranteed survival, food, procreation. The hexagon of the crystal constituted a divine principle of organization, a model of order and continuity. To them, gold and emeralds formed the foundations of a transcendental world view.[32] Even if they *were* a measure of a man's wealth, it was a wealth that belonged to divine forces. We do not share their vision. We never did.

We do appreciate the occasional purity of a golden jewel, its aesthetic appeal, and its exquisite craftsmanship. We admire its technology and are puzzled by its iconography. But there is no way we can recapture its full significance. The deeper meaning is lost forever. Only in our narrow vision of economic wealth, and riches, and power over others can we think of the treasures of El Dorado.

NOTES

1. For background information on the Tukanoan tribes, see, among others, Brüzzi, 1962; Koch-Grünberg, 1909–1910; Reichel-Dolmatoff, 1971, 1975, 1978b, 1978c.
2. On metal adornments, mainly triangular silver pendants, see: Koch-Grünberg, 1905–1910, I, p. 256; Llanos and Pineda, 1978; Roth, 1924. From historical and ethnohistorical sources it seems that metal objects were in use mainly among Arawakan tribes, such as the Caviyarís, Tariana, and their neighbors (Llano and Pineda, 1978). Among the Arawakan Siusí who live to the north of the Vaupés territory, these silver triangles used to be fairly frequent and were called *makálu*, "butterflies," in their language. The Tuyuka Indians of the Tiquié river, a Tukanoan tribe closely related to the Desana, call the triangles *momóno*, also meaning "butterfly," in their respective language (Koch-Grünberg, 1909–1910, I, pp. 85–86, Fig. 42; p. 256, Fig. 138). Roth (1924, p. 436) writes: "*The presence of reptilian shoulderblades alongside these triangular plates is remarkable… as possible examples of adoptation of a natural form.*" (See also, Roth, 1924, pp. 415–417; Plate 147C; pp. 435–436, 574). Brüzzi (1962, p. 314) mentions ear pendants "*…possivelmente de metal dourado…*" in possession of the *Makú* headman at Yavareté, a Salesian Mission station on the middle course of the Vaupés.
3. On color symbolism, see Reichel-Dolmatoff, 1978b.
4. Pheromones are molecules which carry a particular odor.
5. Some expressions are: *nya'pá tuuyágë vaa*, "frog-to join-I go," referring to intercourse; *nya'pá vaagë vaa*, "frog-to split-I go," with the same interpretation.
6. There also exists a relationship with the term *pogá*, "starch, semen, pollen," and *bogá*, "energy."
7. Reichel-Dolmatoff, 1978b, p. 269.
8. On the use of hallucinogenic drugs, by the Desana and their neighbors, see Reichel-Dolmatoff, 1975, 1978c.
9. *Geochelone denticulata.*
10. See Reichel-Dolmatoff, 1978b, pp. 265–271; 1979; 1981a (in press); 198b (in press).
11. From *ëhtaye*, "stone;" *ëhéri*, "to burn, to transform;" *bohóri*, "to reduce, to condense, to concentrate;" *-ru*, a suffix indicating a male, tubular elongated element.
12. Tourmaline occurs in a very wide range of colors which, next to its hexagonal structure, would be one of the main reasons why shamans should attribute to it many energizing properties.
13. Reichel-Dolmatoff, 1978b; 1979.
14. For other illustrations of Tukanoan quartz pendants, see Brüzzi, 1962, p. 312, 336; Koch-Grünberg, 1909–1910, Abb. 206, pp. 242, 326–327; Roth, 1924, Plate 148E, pp. 574–575. Alfred Russel Wallace wrote in the eighteen-fifties: "*I now saw several men with their most peculiar and valued ornament–a cylindrical, opaque, stone, looking like marble, but which is really quartz imperfectly crystallized. The stones are from four to eight inches long, and about an inch in diameter. They are ground round, and flat at the ends, a work of great labour, and are each pierced with a hole at one end, through which a string is inserted, to suspend it around the neck.*" (Wallace, 1972, pp. 191–192).
15. On the Tairona, see Reichel-Dolmatoff, 1951.
16. On the Kogi Indians, see Preuss, 1926; Reichel-Dolmatoff, 1950–1951; 1978a.
17. Reichel-Dolmatoff, 1978a.
18. On jaguar symbolism, see Reichel-Dolmatoff, 1975.
19. For illustrations of Kogi masks, see Preuss, 1926, Figures 22, 23, 26, 30, 31, 33.
20. See also, Mason, 1936, pp. 249–250, Plates CLIX–CLXIII.
21. See, for example, Mason, 1936, p. 156.
22. The expression "to twist cotton thread" conveys an image of sexual connotations which is frequently mentioned in shamanic texts, or in ritual prohibitions (e.g., among the Kogi, Desana, and others).
23. Cortés, 1959, p. 400.
24. On the prehistoric and historic salt trade in Colombia, see Cardale-Schrimpff, 1974. Brine boiling sites have been reported from archaeological excavations in the Central Cordillera, a region where several important chiefdoms flourished in the sixteenth century, all of which had extensive trade relationships (Cardale-Schrimpff, *ibid.*, p. 84).
25. Simon, II, pp. 320–321.
26. Cortés, 1960.
27. Bloch (1976, p. 347) writes: "*The morals associated with salt production are also related to the sexual aspect of mythology. Sexual function is the first to suffer when a man or woman is very salt-hungry. As a result, salt-starved people find salt a strong aphrodisiac. In Cyprus Aphrodite rising from the waves was worshipped both as the Goddess of Love and Salt, her festivities combining a solemn eating of salt with orgiastic rites.*" The Greek biographer Plutarch writes: "*…it is most probable that the salt raises an itching in Animals, and makes them salacious and eager to couple; and perhaps for the same reason they call a surprising and bewitching beauty, such as is apt to move and entice, 'saltish'; and I think that poets had a respect for this generative power of salt in their fable of Aphrodite springing from the sea…*" (Symp. 5, 10, 2, Quaest. conviv. 7, 4, 7).
28. Rock-salt is called *seisháku,* in Kogi, a term related to *téishua* and the complex of words referring to virility and fertility.
29. The Tukanoan tribes burn dry Cecropia leaves and mix the white ashes with powdered coca leaves.
30. Cortés, 1958, p. 400; 1960, *passim.*
31. Eliade (1978, p. 44) writes that in India it was believed that precious stones represented "*a difference in age expressed in embryological terms; the diamond is pakka, i.e. 'ripe,' while the crystal is kaccha, 'not ripe,' 'green,' insufficiently developed. A similar conception was preserved in Europe up to the seventeenth century.*" These beliefs make one wonder about shamanistic ideas concerning the relationship between emeralds and rock crystals. In Muisca territory, the region lying between the Muzo emerald mines and the large rock crystal deposits of the headwaters of the Suarez river, was occupied by many sacred sites, and the present day peasants continue to find caches containing emeralds and rock crystals. It is significant that this region constitutes, since the sixteenth century, a center of Catholic shrines and pilgrimage circuits.
32. It is characteristic that Colombian Indians hardly ever manufactured tools or weapons from metal. The golden needles, fishhooks, tweezers, or other apparently utilitarian objects which have been found, probably had ritual functions. But there are no axes, projectile points, or knives; only a few copper chisels may have served practical purposes.

BIBLIOGRAPHY

Bloch, M. R.
1976   Salt in Human History. *Interdisciplinary Science Reviews,* Vol. 1, No. 4, pp. 336–352.

Brüzzi Alves da Silva, Alcionilio
1962   A civilização indigena do Uaupás. São Paulo.

Cardale-Schrimpff, Marianne
1975   Prehistoric Salt Production in Colombia, South America. In: Salt: The Study of an Ancient Industry. *Report on the Salt Weekend held at the University of Essex, 1974,* p. 84.

Castellanos, Juan de
1850   Elegías de Varones Ilustres de Indias. Biblioteca de Autores Españoles, segunda edición, Rivadeneyra, Madrid.

Cortés, Vicenta
1959   Objetos votivos de la Provincia de Tunja. *Actas del XXXIII Congreso Internacional de Americanistas, San José, 1958,* Vol. II, pp. 398–402. San José de Costa Rica.

Cortés Alonso, Vicenta
1960   Visita a los santuarios indígenas de Boyacá en 1577. *Revista Colombiana de Antropología,* Vol. IX, pp. 201–273, Bogotá.

Duque Gomez, Luis
1945   Apuntes sobre el comercio entre los indios precolombinos. *Boletín de Arqueología,* Vol. I, No. 1, pp. 31–35, Bogotá.

Eliade, Mircea
1968   The Forge and the Crucible: A Postscript. *History of Religions,* Vol. 8, No. 1, pp. 74–88, University of Chicago, Chicago.

1978   The Forge and the Crucible: The Origins and Structure of Alchemy. University of Chicago Press, Chicago.

Hamlin, A. C.
1873   The Tourmaline. James R. Osgood & Co., Boston.

Koch-Grünberg, Theodor
1909–1910   Zwei Jahre unter den Indianern: Reisen in Nordwest-Brasilien 1903/1905. 2 vols., Ernst Wasmuth, Berlin.

Kunz, George Frederick
1971   The Curious Lore of Precious Stones. Dover Publications, New York.

Lesh, Cheri
1979   Quartz: Myth and Magic, Science and Sales. *Gems and Gemology,* Vol. XVI, No. 6, pp. 174–178, Gemological Institute of America, Santa Monica.

Llanos, V. Hector, and Roberto Pineda C.
  1978   Etnohistoria del bajo Caquetá-Putumayo (s. XVI-XVII-XVIII-XIX). *Boletín del Museo del Oro,* Vol. 1, pp. 55–62, Banco de la República, Bogotá.
Mason, J. Alden
  1931   Archaeology of Santa Marta, Colombia. The Tairona Culture. Part I, Report on Field Work, *Anthropological Series,* Vol. XX, No. 1, Field Museum of Natural History, Chicago.
  1936   Archaeology of Santa Marta, Colombia. The Tairona Culture. Part II, Section 1. Objects of Stone, Shell, Bone, and Metal. *Anthropological Series,* Vol. XX, No. 2, Field Museum of Natural History, Chicago.
  1939   Archaeology of Santa Marta, Colombia. The Tairona Culture. Part II, Section 2. Objects of Pottery. *Anthropological Series,* Vol. XX, No. 3, Field Museum of Natural History, Chicago.
Oviedo y Valdés, Gonzalo Fernández
  1851–
  1855   Historia General y Natural de las Indias Islas y Tierra Firme del Mar Oceano. 4 vol., José Amador de los Ríos, Madrid. See also the undated Asunción edition.
Preuss, Konrad Theodor
  1926   Forschungsreise zu den Kágaba. Beobachtungen, Textaufnahmen und sprachliche Studien bei einem Indianerstamm in Kolumbien, Südamerika. Anthropos Verlag, St. Gabriel-Mödling.

Reichel-Dolmatoff, G.
  1950–
  1951   Los Kogi: Una tribu indigena de la Sierra Nevada de Santa Marta, Colombia. 2 vol., Bogotá.
  1951   Datos histórico-culturales sobre las tribus de la antigua Gobernación de Santa Marta. Bogotá.
  1971   Amazonian Cosmos: The Sexual and Religious Symbolism of the Tukano Indians. University of Chicago Press, Chicago.
  1975   The Shaman and the Jaguar: A Study of Narcotic Drugs Among the Indians of Colombia. Temple University Press, Philadelphia.
  1978a   The Loom of Life: A Kogi Principle of Integration. *Journal of Latin American Lore,* Vol. 4, No. 1, pp. 5–27, University of California, Los Angeles.
  1978b   Desana Animal Categories, Food Restrictions, and the Concept of Color Energies. *Journal of Latin American Lore,* Vol. 4, No. 2, pp. 243–291, University of California, Los Angeles.
  1978c   Beyond the Milky Way: Hallucinatory Imagery of the Tukano Indians. University of California, Latin American Center, Los Angeles.
  1979   Desana Shaman's Rock Crystals and the Hexagonal Universe. *Journal of Latin American Lore,* Vol. 5, No. 1, pp. 117–128, University of California, Los Angeles.
  1981a   Some Source Materials on Desana Shamanistic Initiation: An Exercise in Textual Analysis. *Antropologica,* Fundación La Salle, Instituto Caribe de Antropología y Sociología, Caracas (in print).
  1981b   Astronomical Models of Social Behavior Among some Indians of Colombia. Paper presented at the Conference on Tropical Archaeoastronomy and Ethnoastronomy, New York Academy of Sciences, April, 1981 (in print).
Rupprich, H. (editor)
  1956   Albrecht Dürers schriftlicher Nachlass. Berlin (*Cf.* Vol. I, p. 155).
Simon, Pedro
  1882   Noticias Historiales de la Conquistas de Tierra Firme en las Indias Occidentales. 5 vol., Medardo Rivas, Bogotá.
Wallace, Alfred Russel
  1972   A Narrative of Travels on the Amazon and Rio Negro. Dover Publications, New York (first published 1853).
Wassén, Henry
  1955   Algunos datos del comercio precolombino en Colombia. *Revista Colombiana de Antropología,* Vol. IV, pp. 89–109, Bogotá.

All photographs by the author, except for PLATE 2 for which he expresses his gratitude to the Field Museum of Natural History, Chicago, and in particular to Dr. Donald Collier, Curator Emeritus. The map was drawn by Mary Butler.

Colombian Emeralds: A Historical Sketch

by PETER C. KELLER

At the same time that the Spaniards were expropriating gold from the Indians of Colombia, they were also energetically searching for emeralds. Emeralds were highly regarded by the Indians, largely for their trade, ceremonial and religious value. The Spaniards undoubtedly acquired huge amounts of emerald, although dependable records of emerald export to Spain are unfortunately very sketchy. We do know that the Indians of Colombia traded emeralds from as far north as Mexico and as far south as Chile. By the time the Spanish arrived in the New World in the early sixteenth century, large quantities of emeralds were being utilized by the natives of Peru, Ecuador, Colombia, and Mexico (Ball, 1931), suggesting that mining and trading of emeralds in Colombia had already been under way a considerable time.

Cortez wrote that upon his arrival in Mexico in 1519, he met Montezuma bedecked with fine emeralds. Montesinos, a priest in Peru between 1628 and 1642, wrote that emeralds were among the spoils of the Inca Sinchi Roca when he conquered Cuzco, Ecuador in 1100 A.D. Emeralds were part of the tribute of a great chief Capac of the early Chimu period (1100 B.C.–600 A.D.) of Peru. So many emeralds were sent to Europe from Peru that the Europeans knew of no other New World source for the gems. Pizarro reportedly sent four chests of emeralds from Peru to the King of Spain in 1533. Father Joseph de Acosta wrote (Ball, 1931) that "two chests of emeralds, each weighing at least 100 pounds" were on the ship when he returned from Peru to Europe in 1587.

The Spaniards naturally began to search for the source of these fine emeralds which were of vastly better quality than the emeralds they were used to from Sikait and Zebara, Egypt, and from Salzburg, Austria. Unable to locate the Peruvian source, the Spanish under Gonzalo Jimanez de Quesada began looking in Colombia. Quesada first encountered emeralds at Turqmeque, Boyaca in 1537, which prompted him to send Captain Pedro F. de Valenzuala to find the source. That same year Valenzuala was successful in finding what is now the Chivor Mine, seventy-five kilometers northeast of Bogotá. The source, known as Somondoco, was a well-developed Chibcha mine. The Spanish immediately took over the deposit and began mining operations, using slave Indian labor.

The search for other deposits continued, however, and in 1564 the second major source of Colombian emeralds was discovered about a hundred kilometers north of Bogotá at Santisima Trinidad de los Muzos, now known simply as Muzo. According to Feininger (1970), initial production at Muzo overshadowed Chivor. The second half of the sixteenth century saw unprecedented emerald production based almost entirely on slave Indian labor.

The immediate result of this huge influx of fine emeralds was a glut on the European market and sub-

sequent drop in prices. It was therefore necessary to find new markets for many of these outstanding emeralds. The most willing of these markets was the Mogul nobility of India who eagerly sought large, fine Colombian emerald crystals. As a result, Spain, through already well-developed trade routes, exported huge amounts of rough Colombian emeralds to India where, generally, they were beautifully carved by Mogul craftsmen and worn by nobility, usually sewn on articles of clothing or worn as turban ornaments.

A large percentage of these carved Mogul emeralds were confiscated by the Persians in their sacking of Delhi in 1739 by Nadir Shah and subsequently taken to Persia. One can get an indication of the vast wealth that the Moguls lost to the Persians by examining the Crown Jewels of Iran where many of these emeralds are now found. Meen and Tushingham (1968) examined over a thousand of these emeralds and reported that most were over 10 carats, and some exceeded 300 carats in weight.

One of the finest examples of these Mogul emeralds found in private hands today is simply known as the "Mogul Emerald." This roughly rectangular carved slab is approximately 2 inches by 1½ inches by ⅜ inch in size and weighs 217.8 carats (Caplan, 1968). One side is carved with the typical floral motif popular with the Mogul craftsman. The other side contains a beautifully inscribed Islamic prayer in Arabic calligraphy. It is particularly significant that the prayer includes the date 1695 A.D., which places the stone in the reign of Mogul Emperor Aurangzeb. According to Caplan (1968), the prayer itself "is a prayer to God and the prophets of the Shiah sect which is centered in Persia."

Many of the finest Colombian emeralds of the late sixteenth century found their way to the Royal Courts of Europe. A very fine example of such Royal emeralds is the Smithsonian Institution's "Spanish Inquisition Necklace." This 300-year-old necklace consists of fifteen major emeralds and over 360 mine-cut diamonds and reportedly, was first worn in the Spanish Court and later in the French Court (Dunn, 1975). It is interesting to note that the emeralds which make up the necklace are in the form of cylindrical and hexagonal beads not unlike those found in pre-Columbian artifacts. It is quite possible, and interesting to contemplate, that these emeralds were in fact pre-Columbian beads taken from the Indians and utilized in their original form in a piece of Royal jewelry. The centerpiece of the necklace is a single 24 x 15 mm. emerald bead of the finest quality which is flanked by fourteen fine, but smaller, emeralds. The emeralds are complemented by over 360 mine-cut diamonds, sixteen of which are major stones of either Indian or Brazilian origin. Dunn (1975) points out that "these sixteen stones have been drilled, and the hole is a curved cavity opening on either side of the girdle of the stone."

By the end of the sixteenth century, the inhumane

treatment of the Indians working both the Muzo and Chivor mines had become intolerable, and in September, 1593, a thirty-nine article decree was issued by Antonio Gonzalez of Colombia protecting the Indians (Johnson, 1961). This decree was subsequently followed by several Royal decrees from Spain enforcing the new laws. Unfortunately, these decrees came too late, for much of the Indian labor force had already been killed off by the deplorable conditions in the mines. By the early seventeenth century, production at both Muzo and Chivor declined dramatically. In 1650, the Muzo mines were declared Royal property which caused a further decline in production. By 1675, Chivor had shut down entirely and was totally lost for the next two hundred years. Muzo continued to operate sporadically, but usually uneconomically, for another two hundred years. In 1871, Muzo was declared the National Emerald Domain by the Colombian Government. Since then it has been under strict government control. When the Muzo area was turned into government-controlled property, production of emeralds all but ceased, and lawlessness prevailed. This condition persisted at Muzo until the early 1970s.

Not long after Muzo was declared to be under government control and the subsequent decline in production, Chivor re-entered the emerald picture. In 1888, Don Francisco Restrepo, a Colombian mining engineer, discovered a 300-year-old manuscript in a Dominican convent in Quito, Ecuador (Anderton, 1950). This manuscript described the location of the lost Chivor mine and noted that the mine was located at the only place in the Andes where one could see through a v-shaped cut to the *llanos*, or plains of the Orinoco. With this information, Restrepo set out to find the lost Chivor mines, and succeeded in 1896 (Feininger, 1970). He almost immediately started to develop the mine, but was inhibited by legal entanglements for fifteen years. In 1911, Restrepo went into partnership with a German mining engineer named Fritz Klein and began to work Chivor successfully. In 1913, the Colombian Supreme Court declared that Chivor was exempt from all taxation and obligations to the government and, to this day, Chivor remains the only Colombian emerald mine in private hands. From 1911 to the present day, Chivor has had problems and has changed ownership among European, American and Colombian companies many times. Two of its most famous superintendents have been Peter Rainier, who wrote the novel *Greenfire*, an account of his exploits at Chivor, and Willis F. Bronkie, an American who saved the mines from bankruptcy in the 1950s. Chivor is currently in the hands of the Quintero family, and production to this day is only sporadic.

Chivor emeralds are generally not considered to be of as fine a quality as those from Muzo, but may be less flawed and much "brighter." Chivor also is not known for producing large crystals. One exception to this rule, however, was the discovery of the 632 carat "Patricia Emerald" by a miner named Justo Daza in December, 1920. The "Patricia" is the largest known Chivor emerald crystal and was sold in 1921 for $60,000.00

The main mine at Muzo is worked by bulldozer until the white, emerald-bearing calcite veins are exposed. Then teams of workers under armed guard are brought in to handpick the vein.

(Johnson, 1961). Its location after the sale was unknown until the early 1950s when it was donated anonymously to the American Museum of Natural History in New York. The "Patricia" is on exhibit for this show and is illustrated in this catalog.

One of the finest emerald crystals in the world was found as recently as 1967 at Gachalá about five kilometers southwest of the Chivor mine. The "Gachalá Emerald" weighs 858 carats and is about 2 x 2 x 2 inches in size (Trapp, 1969). The single crystal is of exceptional quality, being a very sharp hexagonal prism with deep green color and very fine luster. George Switzer, former curator of the Smithsonian Institution Gem Collection where the "Gachalá" now resides, stated that the crystal "is the finest example to be seen in any museum in the world today."

Emerald mining under Colombian government control has been a questionable business. The government was unable to make money mining at Muzo during the first half of the twentieth century. In 1946, the government handed over the management of Muzo to the Banco de la República, the National Bank. The bank supervised Muzo until 1969. During this period, several emeralds of major importance were discovered and placed in the vaults of the bank in Bogotá where they remain to this day. There are five major emeralds weighing 1759.0 carats, 1795.85 carats, 1482.5 carats, 1,020.5 carats, and 220.0 carats. Of these five crystals, two are of exceptional quality; the 1,020.5 carat crystal and the 1759.0 carat crystal. The 1759.0 carat 50 x 45 x 89 mm crystal may, in fact, be the largest very fine rough emerald crystal in the world. As a collection these crystals are comparable with the best emerald crystal collections known.

The five emerald crystals are, for the most part, characteristically simple hexagonal prisms with most second order prism development. The 1795.85 carat crystal and the 1482.5 carat crystal have a definite blue-green appearance generally associated with the Chivor mine, although all the crystals in the Bank Collection

A group of 'guaqueros' in the streambed at Muzo, Colombia.

are reputedly from Muzo. The crystals have interesting rectangular etch faces and minor calcite inclusions and some associated pyrite.

This period since 1947 produced, in addition to the five crystals in the Banco de la República, the largest Colombian emerald crystal in the world: the 7025 carat "Emilia Emerald" from the Las Cruces mine. The crystal is of poorer quality than those in the collection in the Bank, but the size is certainly extraordinary. It has been displayed at various expositions around the world since its discovery in 1969 by a private mining concern. Its current whereabouts are unknown.

One of the finest cut emeralds produced in the twentieth century is the 75 carat square-cut "Hooker Emerald." This magnificent stone is surprisingly free of the internal flaws usually characteristic of an emerald of this size, and is of the finest color. As with the "Spanish Inquisition Necklace" and the "Gachalá Emerald," the "Hooker" is part of the gem collection of the Smithsonian Institution. Both the Inquisition Necklace and the "Hooker Emerald" are part of the current exhibition, and are pictured in the color plates of this catalog.

The situation for increased production of emeralds in Colombia is now more encouraging than it has been for over two hundred years. In 1977, the Colombian Government solicited bids from private mining concerns to mine the Muzo area. These five-year leases were awarded to Colombian companies, and the increased production has been staggering. In 1973, Colombia re-

ported two million dollars in emerald exports. In 1978, the year that the private mining commenced, exports rose to forty million dollars. In just the first seven months of 1979, this figure almost doubled to seventy-five million dollars in emerald exports from Colombia (Baskin, 1979). With this increased activity, we should soon see some major new emeralds appear in the marketplace. One hopes that these crystals will ultimately reside in the public museums of the world for all to enjoy.

BIBLIOGRAPHY

Anderton, R. W., 1950, Report on Chivor Emerald Mine: Gems and Gemology, v. 6, pp. 276–277.

Ball, S. H., 1931, Historical Notes on Gem Mining: Economic Geology, v. 26, pp. 681–738.

Baskin, G. D., 1979, Gemstones, in U.S. Bureau of Mines Minerals Yearbook: p. 9.

Caplan, A., 1968, An Important Carved Emerald from the Mogul Period of India, Lapidary Journal, v. 22, pp. 1336–1337.

Dunn, P., 1975, Emeralds in the Smithsonian Gem Collection: Lapidary Journal, v. 29, pp. 1572–1575.

Feininger, T., 1970, Emerald Mining in Colombia: History and Geology, The Mineralogical Record, v. 1, pp. 142–149.

Johnson, P. W., 1961, The Chivor Emerald Mine, Journal of Gemology, v. 8, no. 4, pp. 126–152.

Trapp, F. W., 1969, The Gachala Emerald Shares the Spotlight with the Hope Diamond at the Smithsonian: Lapidary Journal, v. 23, no. 4, p. 628.

Ancient Gold Pectorals from Colombia: Mushroom Effigies? by RICHARD EVANS SCHULTES and ALEC BRIGHT

One of the most fascinating and enigmatic archaeological objects in the Americas is a certain type of anthropomorphic gold pectoral found in southern Panama and, most especially, in Colombia. Called "Darien pectorals," these ornaments are not confined to one region, although their greatest concentration seems to be in the Sinú country in northwestern Colombia, near the border with Panama's Darien Province. They are found also in the Quimbaya region of Colombia, farther south.

The dating of the Colombian gold objects and the styles of these objects are still rather indefinite, although archaeologists would generally place Sinú and Quimbaya goldwork in the late pre-Columbian centuries, most likely in the span of 1,000–1,500 A.D., but with the possibility of beginnings as early as 500 A.D.

Interestingly, one such "Darien pectoral" has been found as far north as Chichen Itzá in Yucatán, where it undoubtedly found its way as an item of long-distance trade, along with other lower Central American and Colombian gold artifacts. The Maya centre of Chichen Itzá—and its famed cenote of sacrifice, where such gold objects were thrown as offerings—was particularly active between 1,000 and 1,250 A.D. This, however, does not help in placing the manufacturing date of the object in question, as many of the other objects found in the Chichen Itzá cenote were clearly heirloom pieces (Willey, pers. comm.).

Although they vary slightly, these ornaments all follow a general plan. They are anthropomorphic, usually highly stylized. The most prominent feature is the pair of dome-shaped or rounded objects arranged side by side on the head. Lateral wing-like ornaments with spiral decorations made up of double spirals almost invariably frame the head of the pectoral. A flat face or mask, sometimes more or less natural but usually with complex filigree ornamentation, is discernible. Arms and hands hold two sticks or wands usually in an inverted V-shape. A frog or toad, sometimes very natural but usually extremely stylized, is almost always present immediately beneath the face: that is, on the chest.

These pectorals have been divided into two general types: "Darien pectorals" and "Darien-related pectorals." The former are the more typical, with most of the principal diagnostic features; the latter have very stylistic variations and fewer of the main diagnostic features, diverting in one or several ways from the basic morphological pattern of the Darien type.

Although a few specimens are to be found in private collections and in several museums, the greatest concentration of these gold pectorals is preserved in the Museo del Oro in Bogotá, Colombia. Thanks to the director, Dr. Luis Duque Gómez, we have had the opportunity of examining in great detail the Museum's collection of more than 150 specimens and of conferring with Mrs. Ana María Falchetti de Sáenz, whose meticulous research is embodied in her thesis entitled *The Goldwork of the Sinú Region, (Northern) Colombia* (Falchetti-Sáenz, 1976).

Because of the two dome-like objects on the head, these pectorals have popularly been called "telephone-bell gods." This term originated apparently from the description given by Dr. José Pérez de Barrada in 1954, when he mentioned "the semi-spherical buttons to which I have referred that remind one of the bells of old fashioned telephones or of a pair of mushrooms" (Pérez, 1954).

Following the intense ethnomycological activities of Dr. R. Gordon Wasson (Wasson, 1962, 1968, 1972, 1979, 1980), his late wife Dr. Valentina P. Wasson (Wasson and Wasson, 1957), and the late Professor Roger Heim (Heim, 1967, 1978; Heim and Wasson, 1958) unveiling the ancient and the contemporary religious use of hallucinogenic mushrooms in southern Mexico, Pérez de Barrada wrote: "It would not be strange to reconsider with great reserve this casual attribution. It should be noted that these semi-spherical buttons are not fixed directly to the head but are attached by means of filaments soldered to the back of the piece...We know nothing about the ritual use of mushrooms amongst the Indians of Darien at the time of the discovery, nor later, but if we remember, but keep it in mind, since no trace was found in the indigenous pharmacopoea of the Catios of the Golfo de Urabá, notwithstanding the excellent monograph by Father Severino Santa Teresa. On the other hand, the secrecy with which these Indians guard their knowledge of the properties of plants and their shamanistic ceremonies could have hidden a possible use of hallucinogenic mushrooms—a use which might be very ancient and which possibly existed in distinct forms. The bridge between Guatemala and Darien is difficult to establish but easy to suspect. Our suggestion that these buttons represent mushrooms is accepted by A. Emmerich" (Pérez, 1954).

This reference to Emmerich leads us directly to the second mention in the literature that these dome-like objects represent mushrooms. "It appears likely that the puzzling, hitherto unidentified hemi-spherical headdress ornaments in fact represent a pair of mushrooms, probably of hallucinogenic properties. It is significant that such mushrooms are to this day traditionally counted, ceremonially used and consumed in pairs...the mushroom head dress ornaments were hammered out separately, riveted to short stems and then soldered to the body" (Emmerich, 1965). (In a note, Emmerich states: "I am indebted to Mrs. Mary U. Light for her original insight in identifying these ornaments as mushrooms.")

A third consideration of the "telephone bell gods" as mushroom effigies was offered in 1974 by Professor Peter T. Furst. Referring to Emmerich, he reported:

"André Emmerich developed the interesting theory that the pairs of telephone bell-like, semi-spherical, hollow-stemmed ornaments surmounting the headdress of a certain class of conventionalized anthropomorphic gold pectorals in the Darién style from Colombia ("telephone gods") are in fact mushrooms. Emmerich demonstrated convincingly that, over time, these ornaments gradually changed position as the effigies themselves became more and more stylized. On early, more realistic pieces, the mushroom form is unmistakable, the semi-spherical caps being separated from the headdress by stems or stipes attached to the top of the head. Subsequently, the stipes became shorter and the caps were slightly inclined forward. Eventually, the stipes, though still present beneath the cap, disappeared altogether from view and the two caps faced forward like a pair of female breasts. By this time the human characters had also been stylized to the point of abstraction" (Furst, 1974, 1976).

Our own studies of the many gold pectorals in the Museo del Oro and our familiarity with the complexities of magico-religious, shamanic or ceremonial use of hallucinogenic plants, together with consideration of the natural range of psilocybine-containing genera of mushrooms in the New World, lead us to the belief that this identification of the dome-shaped headdress ornaments is indeed correct and that, further, they strongly suggest the religious use in prehispanic Colombia of intoxicating mushrooms. This interpretation of the gold pectorals has already twice been supported (Schultes and Hofmann, 1979, 1980).

No other explanation of the possible significance of these domes has ever, so far as we know, been advanced. Significance they most certainly must have had. We are left, then, with the inescapable conclusion that they cannot represent anything else than mushrooms.

In a number of the pectorals, the domes are elevated on a stipe. Furthermore, a few of the domes have a mammiform tip characteristic of some species of *Psilocybe,* and several have a design along the margin of the cap which could be interpreted as indicative of the scalloped edge of the cap of *Panaeolus sphinctrinus.* We have, in addition, several tangential arguments which have not hitherto been offered and which, we believe, lend weight to this interpretation.

As with the intoxications induced by many hallucinogens, levitation—the sensation of flying or soaring through the air and visiting distant places — is a commonly experienced psychic effect of psilocybine, the principal active constituent of species of *Panaeolus, Psilocybe* and *Stropharia* (Schultes and Hofmann, 1979; Brown, 1972).

In her long and involved chant during the Mazatec mushroom ceremony, for example, the famous shaman María Sabina repeatedly sings such descriptive phrases as "Whirling woman am I," "Look, I feel as though I'm going to the sky," "Woman like the big eagle am I,"

"Woman of space am I" (Halifax, 1979). Dr. Albert Hofmann, the chemist who first isolated psilocybine and psilocine from the sacred mushrooms and who elucidated their structures and synthesized them, mentions levitation amongst other symptoms produced by small doses of psilocybine: "...bodily relaxation and detachment from the environment...effects...associated with a pleasant feeling of extraordinary lightness, a bodily hovering" (Schultes and Hofmann, 1979, 1980). Wasson, the first to provide a detailed description of psilocybine-mushroom intoxication, reported specifically, amongst many other effects, the experience of levitation: "...the bemushroomed person is poised in space, a disembodied eye, invisible, incorporeal, seeing but not seen...your body lies in darkness, heavy as lead, but your spirit seems to soar...and with the speed of thought to travel where it listeth, in time and space..." (Schultes, 1973).

The Colombian gold pectorals almost invariably have two wings formed by spirals and arising at an angle lateral to the headdress ornaments. They vary somewhat in shape but always involve spiral filagree work. While occasionally abbreviated, they are usually elongated. We believe that these represent wings, the wings of a mythical bird, and are directly associated with levitation. Furthermore, we need not detail how frequently and how generally, not only in the Americas but in the Old World as well, are birds associated with hallucinogens, but several examples will suffice.

Amongst the Koryaks of Siberia, the culture hero, Big Raven, discovered the hallucinogenic mushroom *Amanita muscaria* from the spittle of the god Vihiyinin (Schultes and Hofmann, 1980). The mythical Thunder Bird carries the prayers of the peyote-eating Indians of the United States to heaven (LaBarre, 1938), and levitation is important in the Huichol peyote ritual in Mexico (Furst and Anguiano, 1977). In eastern Brazil, the Indians who drank *vinho de jurema (Mimosa hostilis)* flew all night carried on the back of a huge bird that skirted thundering rapids and showed its passengers the abodes of the dead (Gonçalves de Lima, 1946).

In several "Darien-related pectorals," the hands hold a bar on which are perched four birds. In one of the pectorals, the birds are movable. We suggest that, in these examples, too, the avian ornamentation indicates association with the flying sensation experienced in mushroom intoxication.

But there is an even more compelling argument for the hallucinogenic connection of the pectorals: the frog or toad. Almost all of the pectorals are ornamented with these amphibian figures. In some cases, the figure is realistic; in others, it is flat but easily discernible—with eyes, legs and a median dorsal band, indicating undoubtedly the coloured band on some of these animals. In most, however, it is highly stylized, their eyes and legs represented by circles of double spirals, the tail portion indicated by a flat triangular projection, and the snout represented occasionally by a knob-like protuberance.

This extraordinarily constant association of the frog or toad with the pectorals would seem to have deep

PLATES 1–4. Colombian gold "mushroom" pectorals showing more or less realistic amphibian forms. Museo del Oro, Bogotá.

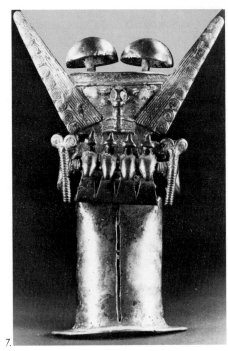

PLATES 5–6. Colombian gold "mushroom" pectorals showing
highly stylized amphibian forms. Museo del Oro, Bogotá.

significance. No other animals represent change and transition more sharply with their dramatic metamorphosis and fertility — passing from the egg to a wholly water-living, gill-breathing creature resembling a fish to a terrestrial, four-legged amphibian. Furthermore, certain frogs of the Dendrobatidae are frighteningly toxic— one species producing the most highly poisonous substance known (Daly and Myers, 1967; Daly and Witkop, 1971). For millenniums and in widely separated parts of the globe, frogs and toads have been associated with origin myths, mysticism, rain and fecundity, the moon, magic and, especially, with intoxication from hallucinogenic agents (Wasson, 1980). This significance of the toad-frog motif has been emphasized by Furst (Furst, 1974, 1976) who succinctly states: "...there is clearly much more than only the 'obvious' connection with rain to account for the importance of the toad-frog motif in the indigenous symbolic system..." (Furst, 1979).

Hallucinogenic constituents found in plants employed for their psychoactive properties have been isolated from frogs and toads. The alkaloid bufotenine, known from the leguminous tree *Anadenanthera peregrina* from which a highly psychoactive snuff is prepared in South America (Holmstedt and Lindgren, 1967), is present in the skin glands of *Bufo marinus* and other amphibians (Schultes and Holmstedt, 1968). The related and more potent hallucinogen, 5-methoxy-N, N-dimethyltryptamine, one of the active components of the snuff prepared in South America from several species of *Virola* trees (Schultes and Holmstedt, 1968), has recently been found in the North American desert toad, *Bufo alvarius* (Furst, 1974). Extremely toxic substances occur in the skin of some species of *Phyllobates* and *Dendrobates*, colourful amphibians of northwes-

ternmost South America in the general region where the gold pectorals are found in greatest concentration. The venoms of some South American frogs and toads are employed in magical contexts, sometimes producing even ecstatic or hallucinogenic states. It was the Swedish anthropologist S. Henry Wassén who, many years ago, reviewed the literature and concluded "...that the ubiquitous frog/toad motif in South American mythology and art, including the great number of effigies of cast gold from pre-Hispanic Colombia and Panama, was inseparable from the practical use of frog venom for blowgun dart poison (which in any event had a magical component) and from the widespread magico-religious beliefs and practices involving the toxins of different species of these amphibians" (Wassen, 1934). Frog poison — probably from a species of *Phyllobates* or *Dendrobates* — is used by hunters among the Amahuaca Indians of Amazonian Peru for inducing hallucinations: the poison is rubbed on self-inflicted cuts, inducing a violent illness, characterized by vomiting, diarrhea, convulsions, unconsciousness. Supernatural expertness in the hunt results from the hallucinations which are interpreted as communication with forest spirits (Furst, 1974).

There can no longer be any doubt that the high place occupied in magico-religious spheres by frogs and toads must be attributed in great part to the toxic properties of some species. Although the potently poisonous South American species cannot be termed hallucinogenic in the usual sense of that word, their toxins do act upon the central nervous system with effects so unreal as to induce the Indian to ascribe supernatural powers to the animal, and actually visual and other hallucinations may indeed accompany the violent intoxications

PLATES 7–8. Colombian gold "mushroom" pectorals showing four avian figures. Museo del Oro, Bogotá.

PLATES 9–10. Views of the back of Colombian gold "mushroom" pectorals showing "stipes" of the mushroom-like domes. Museo del Oro, Bogotá.

caused by agents that can in no wise be considered true hallucinogens (Furst, 1974, 1976). For, as has been correctly pointed out: "...the massive assault on the system brought on by bufotenine-containing *Bufo* venom is of a very different order than the shift from one state of consciousness to another triggered by bufotenine-containing snuff" (Furst, 1974). Perhaps it may not be wholly coincidental that toads were so frequently added as an ingredient of the hallucinogenic witches brews of medieval Europe.

Whether as hallucinogen-inducing organisms, or as poisonous animals causing what might be termed pseudohallucination syndromes, these amphibians assumed—for this and other peculiarities—a significance in aboriginal mythology and magic, and an exalted position amongst the peoples who created the Colombian gold work.

In almost every gold-working culture of Colombia, there are numerous examples of the toad-frog motif. There are hundreds of specimens in the Museo del Oro in Bogotá. These are especially abundant in the Tairona area of the Sierra Nevada de Santa Marta. From the surviving aboriginal groups of Indians still living in this region, it is known that the frog is considered a mythological being at the center of the cosmos (Reichel-Dolmatoff, 1963).

We believe that, especially when other characteristics of the gold pectorals (wings, birds, mushrooms) are taken into account, the constancy of the frog-toad motif on these artifacts must of necessity be interpreted as an indication that they played some role in a magico-religious system based on the hallucinatory experience. That no reference to the hallucinogenic use of mushrooms amongst the Indians of Colombia is found in the writings of the Spanish conquerors hardly argues against the possibility of such employment: the use and the cults connected with the mushrooms may well have died out between the dates of the latest gold pectorals and the sixteenth century.

It would, of course, be a futile exercise to presume that the gold pectorals in question—or any other artifact, for that matter—represent the use of hallucinogenic mushrooms, unless mushrooms possessing psychotomimetic constituents actually do occur in the region where the artifacts were made and used.

Although the collection and study of mushrooms in Colombia is still in a very preliminary stage, psilocybine-containing species have been reported. Species of *Psilocybe* are known to be widely distributed in the world, and the field studies of Dr. Gastón Guzmán in 1964 and 1971 have indicated that hallucinogenic species of *Psilocybe* occur in Colombia (Guzmán and Varela, 1978). The localities are widely distributed throughout the nation and vary from the warm lowlands to *páramos* at high elevation. According to Guzmán, the following species of *Psilocybe* have been registered from Colombia: *P. antillarum* (Fr.) Quél., *P. argentina* (Speg.) Sing., *P. bullacea* (Bull. ex Fr.) Kumm., *P. columbia* Guzmán, *P. Pintonii* Guzmán and *P. subcubensis* Guzmán (which is occasionally considered to be a variant of *Stropharia cubensis*). A number of these mushrooms are presumably psilocybine-containing, since they are cyanescent and have a farinaceous odor and taste — indicative, according to Guzmán's experience, that they are hallucinogenic. Furthermore, *Panaeolus sphinctrinus* (Fr.) Bresadola, known as one of the hallucinogenic mushrooms of Mexico, has been collected in Colombia (Guzmán and Varela, 1978).

41

Guzmán writes in a letter: "I agree with you that the South American Indians used hallucinogenic species of *Psilocybe*. I reported thirty species from South America, but I think that there are more, but we need more explorations. Even I think that the Indians from the Atlantic zone and not only those of the Andes used the hallucinogenic mushrooms." The recent field work of Dr. Kenneth Dumont has resulted in the registration from Colombia of other species of *Psilocybe*, a number of which may likewise be psilocybine-containing (Dumont, pers. comm.).

Our studies of the Darien and Darien-related gold pectorals of Colombia have strengthened our belief that mushrooms perhaps enjoyed a widespread magico-religious place in aboriginal cultures from Mexico, through Central America and in the Andes south to Peru.

There are many pieces of evidence that may be interpreted as supporting such a belief. One manifestation of this cultural trait is provided by the numerous "mushroom stones" of Mexico, Guatemala and El Salvador, which have been extensively studied and documented (Borhegyi, 1957, 1961; Wasson, 1957; Rose, 1977). Four of these stone figures significantly have a frog-figure at their base (Wasson, 1980). Further south in Mexico and extending southeastward to El Salvador are various ceramic representations which have been interpreted as mushroom-related artifacts. From Colombia, there is one ceramic object from the area of greatest concentration of gold Darien pectorals which, although far less convincing than the gold objects, might be interpreted as representing a mushroom, since it has an undulating "cap" which occurs in some species of *Psilocybe*. There are, furthermore, numerous clay artifacts from Mexico with representations of mushrooms in contexts suggestive of their significance in magico-religious rituals (Borhegyi, 1963; Furst, 1974).

PLATE 11. *Two of the rare Colombian gold "mushroom" pectorals showing three (instead of two) dome-shaped objects at the top. Museo del Oro, Bogotá.*

We might also mention at this point that several unusual "mushroom-like" ceramic pieces have been excavated at Araracuara in the Colombian Amazon (Herrera, pers. comm.).

Further to the south in the Andes, ceramic pots in the form of a human head with a mushroom-like protuberance from the forehead are frequent in the Mochica. This protuberance could not function as a handle: if the pot were filled with liquid, it would be too heavy to be supported by such a brittle handle. To the best of our knowledge, no functional explanation of this type of protuberance has been offered. They are all in shape very suggestive of mushrooms. One of the pots figured actually has painted flecks on the cap which might lead one to suspect that it represents *Amanita muscaria*, even though the species is believed not to have existed this far south in pre-Columbian times. These and other pottery artifacts, considered in detail by Furst (Furst, 1974), tend to support the belief that mushrooms were important in pre-Columbian art in more than one locality in the Andes of South America.

It has only recently been discovered that the fly agaric, *Amanita muscaria*, has deep-rooted religious significance and is still ceremonially used by the Ojibway Indians living on Lake Superior in the United States (Wasson, 1979) and that Indians of the Mackensie River

PLATE 12. *Seated man, Colombian Quimbaya Culture, gold. Note the two mushroom-like objects on the head and the two bird (toucan?) beaks in place of legs.*

area of British Columbia, Canada, similarly employ this hallucinogen (Halifax, pers. comm.).

It is possibly significant that the Mackensie River area, being largely glacier-free in the Pleistocene, may have been one of the main routes taken by early man on his migrations from Siberia to the Americas.

Perhaps it may not be superfluous, in closing, to point out that from Asia ancient mythological ideas stemming from the use of hallucinogenic mushrooms and their concomitant associations are traceable in European witchcraft, in the cult of soma in the Indian subcontinent, in the use of fly agaric in Siberia and at least in two contemporary and unrelated and widely separated indigenous groups in North America.

In view of the recognized widespread magicoreligious use of mushrooms in the New World, we believe that the interpretation of the Colombian "telephone bell gods," as mushroom-related artifacts, represents perhaps the most plausible explanation thus far advanced and that it may be of the utmost importance in our studies of the role of hallucinogens in aboriginal societies of the New World.

ACKNOWLEDGMENTS

Permission to publish the plates graciously has been given by Dr. Luis Duque Gómez, Director, Museo del Oro, Bogotá, Colombia. We gratefully acknowledge permission to publish plate 12 which has been granted by the Cleveland Museum of Art, Cleveland, Ohio (gift of Mr. and Mrs. R. Henry Norweb). We thank the director of the Peabody Museum, Harvard University, Prof. Clifford Lamberg-Karlovsky, for permission to reproduce plates 10 and 11 (Photograph by Hillel Burger).

REFERENCES

Borhegyi, S. F. De, "Mushroom stones of Middle America. A geographically and chronologically arranged distribution chart" in V. P. and R. G. Wasson, Mushrooms, Russia and History. Pantheon, New York 2 (1957) Appendix.

Borhegyi, S. F. De, "Miniature mushroom stones from Guatemala" in Am. Antiq. 26(1961) 498–504.

Borhegyi, S. F. De, "Pre-Columbian pottery mushrooms from Mesoamerica" in Am. Antiq. 28(1963) 328–338.

Brown, F. C. Hallucinogenic Drugs. Charles C. Thomas, Springfield, Ill. (1972) 80.

Daly, J. W. and C. W. Myers, "Toxicity of Panamanian poison frogs (Dendrobates): some biological and chemical aspects" in Science 156(1967) 970 1973.

Daly, J. W. and B. Witkop, "Chemistry and pharmacology of frog venoms" in W. Bucheri, E. E. Buckley and V. Deulofeu (Eds.) Venomous Animals and their Venoms. Academic Press, New York (1971) 497–519.

Dumont, K. Personal communication.

Emmerich, A. Sweat of the Sun and Tears of the Moon. University of Washington Press, Seattle, Wash. (1965).

Falchetti de Sáenz, A. M. The Goldwork of the Sinú Region, (Northern) Colombia. University of London (Unpubl. Thesis) (1976).

Falchetti de Sáenz, A. M., "Colgantes 'Darien'" in Bol. Mus. Oro 2(1979) 1–55.

Furst, P. T., "Hallucinogens in pre-Columbian art" in Spec. Publ. Mus. Texas Technical University 7(1974) 55–102.

Furst, P. T., Hallucinogens and Culture. Chandler and Sharp Publishers, San Francisco (1976).

Furst, P. T. and M. Anguiano, "'To fly as birds': myth and ritual as agents of enculturation among Huichol Indians of Mexico" in J. Wilbert (Ed.) Enculturation in Latin America: an Anthology. UCLA Latin American Center Publications, University of California, Los Angeles (1977) 95–181.

Gonçalves de Lima, O., "Observações sôbre o vinho da jurema utilizado pelos indios Pancarú de Tacaratú (Pernambuco)" in Arqu. Inst. Pesquisas Agron. 4(1946) 45–80.

Guzmán, G. and L. Varela, "Hongos de Colombia III" in Caldasia 12(1978) 309–338.

Guzmán-Huerta, G., Estudio Taxonómico y Ecológico de los Hongos Neutrópicos Mexicanos. Tésis Profesional, Instituto Politécnico Nacional, Ciencias Biológicas, Mexico (1959).

Halifax, J., Shamanic Voices. E. P. Dutton, New York (1979).

Halifax, J., Personal communication.

Harner, M.J., "Common themes in South American Indian yajé experiences" in M. J. Harner (Ed.) Hallucinogens and Shamanism. Oxford University Press, New York (1963) 155–175.

Heim, R., Nouvelles Investigations sur les Champignons Hallucinogenes. Museum National d'Histoire Naturelle, Paris (1967).

Heim, R., Les Champignons Toxiques et Hallucinogènes (Ed. 2) Société Nouvelle des Editions Boubée, Paris (1978).

Heim, R. and R. G. Wasson, Les Champignons Hallucinogènes du Mexique. Museum National d'Histoire Naturelle, Paris (1958).

Herrera, W. Personal communication.

Hofmann, A., LSD-Mein Sorgenkind. Klett-Cotta, Stuttgart (1979).

Holmstedt, B. and J.-E. Lindgren, "Chemical constituents and pharmacology of South American snuffs" in D. H. Efron (Ed.) Ethnopharmacologic Search for Psychoactive Drugs, Public Health Service Publ. No. 1645, U.S. Government Printing Office, Washington, D.C. (1967) 339–373.

LaBarre, W., The Peyote Cult. Yale University Publications in Anthropology, New Haven, Conn. (1938).

Pérez de Barradas, J., Orfebrería Prehispánica de Colombia: Estilo Calima. Gráficos Jura, Madrid (1954).

Reichel-Dolmatoff, G., "Apuntes etnográficos sobre los indios del alto Rio Sinú" in Rev. Acad. Col. Cienc. Exact., Fis. Nat. 12, no. 45(1963) 29–40.

Rose, R. M., Mushroom Stones of Mesoamerica. Unpubl. Ph.D. Thesis, Harvard University, Cambridge, Mass. (1977).

Schultes, R. E., "An overview of hallucinogens in the Western Hemisphere" in P. T. Furst (Ed.) Flesh of the Gods. Praeger, New York (1972) 28.

Schultes, R.E., Hallucinogenic Plants. Golden Press, New York (1976).

Schultes, R. E. and A. Hofmann, The Botany and Chemistry of Hallucinogens. Ed. 2 Charles C. Thomas, Springfield, Ill. (1979).

Schultes, R. E. and A. Hofmann, Plants of the Gods: Origins of Hallucinogenic Use. McGraw Hill Co., New York (1980).

Schultes, R. E. and B. Holmstedt, "De plantis toxicariis e Mundo Novo tropicale commentationes II. The vegetal ingredients of the myristicaceous snuffs of the northwest Amazon" in Rhodora 70 (1968) 113–160.

Wassén, S. H., "The frog-motive among South American Indians" in Anthropos 29(1934) 319–370. "Part II. The frog in Indian mythology and imaginative world" Ibid., 613–658.

Wasson, R. G., "The hallucinogenic mushrooms of Mexico and psilocybine: a bibliography" in Bot. Mus. Leafl. Harvard Univ. 20(1962) 25–73.

Wasson, R. G., Soma-Divine Mushroom of Immortality. Harcourt, Brace and World, New York (1968).

Wasson, R. G., "The divine mushroom of immortality" in P. T. Furst (Ed.) Flesh of the Gods. Praeger Publishers, New York (1972) 185–200.

Wasson, R. G., "Traditional use in North America of Amanita muscaria for divinatory purposes" in Journ. Psyched. Drugs 11(1979) 25–28.

Wasson, R.G., The Wondrous Mushroom: Mycolatry in Mesoamerica. McGraw Hill, New York (1980).

Wasson, V. P. and R. G. Wasson, Mushrooms, Russia and History. Pantheon, New York (1957).

Willey, G. R., Personal communication.

Technology of Pre-Columbian Gold Working

by PETER T. FURST

Most students of metal working agree that the goldsmiths of ancient America, with a few exceptions, such as electroplating and enameling, mastered nearly all of the techniques of their craft still known and used today.

They worked with gold, tin, silver, copper, lead and even platinum, and with alloys of two or more of these. Iron, of course, was unknown before the coming of the Spaniards. Their techniques included hammering and embossing; hammering on molds; stretching and shaping with repeated annealing; soldering, sheathing and inlaying; casting in open and closed molds of both solid and hollow objects of the greatest intricacy; plating and many others. They were able even to achieve the effect of several colors on the surface of alloys by treating them with acids to dissolve the baser metals. And although steel graving tools were lacking, fine designs were achieved which closely resemble engraving.

No wonder, then, that the great goldsmith of the Italian Renaissance, Benvenuto Cellini, as well as the German master Albrecht Dürer, expressed themselves in superlatives in describing the delicate craftsmanship and extraordinary beauty of the first objects of precious metal to reach the Old World from newly-discovered America.

What is all the more remarkable is that the high degree of technical proficiency and aesthetic quality evidenced by the objects themselves is not matched by the equipment at the disposal of the ancient American goldsmiths. The finished pieces presuppose some knowledge of mining techniques and the properties of various metals, as well as the use of certain indispensable tools, such as furnaces and some means of blasting— or forcing air into the fire — in addition to hammers, anvils, crucibles and tools for the handling of red-hot metals. All of these were, indeed, present, but all were of the simplest kind.

Gold, it seems, was panned or collected in the form of nuggets and perhaps dust, sometimes in a series of stone riffles constructed across stream beds. There are reports of some form of hydraulic mining as well: cliffs are said to have been undercut and hillsides washed away by running water from reservoirs and canals against them. Fire and water were used to splinter ore-bearing rocks and brush is said to have been burned on hills to melt silver in exposed veins — at least that is the report of some chroniclers. The Spaniards also speak of pre-Conquest gold mines, but proof of these is scant, nor is it known at present whether gold was ever actually smelted from auriferous ores. In any event, pits seem to have been of the open variety, and rarely deep.

Religious beliefs and observances were also involved in the mining and collection of metals; according to Father Cobo's *Historia del Nuevo Mundo*, the ore-bearing hills in the Inca realm were regarded as sacred and referred to as "coya," the Quechua term for queen, and all-night ceremonies held to propitiate them. The precious metal in the rock, according to this account, was addressed by the kinship term "Mama," the same word used by Quechua-speakers to address their own mothers and maternal aunts in Inca times. (In Mexico, where metal working appeared much later, gold and goldsmiths were also surrounded by a strong religious aura.)

To return to technology: Peruvian anvils were of the simplest kind. The chronicler Garcilaso de la Vega speaks of flattened stones of great hardness which served the metal worker as anvils, but points out that hammers with handles were unknown in ancient Peru. Instead, he describes the use of bronze cubes with rounded corners which, held in the hand "as if they were pebbles," served as hammer substitutes. Stone and metal objects fitting this description have been found.

Nor did the metal workers of ancient America have the benefit of bellows for blast furnaces. Again we draw on the Royal Commentaries of Garcilaso de la Vega:

"They blasted by means of tubes of copper, the length of half-a-cubit, more or less, according as the furnace was large or small. The tubes were closed at one end, leaving one small hole through which the air could rush with more force. As many as eight, ten or twelve of these were put together, according to the requirements of the furnace; and they went round the fire blowing the tubes."

Metal tongs were likewise unknown. Garcilaso states that the metal was taken red hot from the fire with "poles of wood or copper," which might be comparable to using a chopstick in each hand to pick up morsels of food in a Chinese restaurant.

"Notwithstanding these inconvenient contrivances," he continues, *"they executed marvellous works.... They also found out...that the smoke of certain metals was injurous to health, and they consequently made their foundries in the open air, in their yards and courts, and never under a roof."*

From our point of view, it is difficult to understand the "failure" (if such it was) of the Peruvians to invent either hammer or tongs in view of their seemingly obvious utility in the handling and working of metals. Certainly *we* would consider them indispensable. Moreover, the Peruvians did have war clubs with stone or metal heads, as well as ingenious one-piece, springy metal tweezers of varying sizes to remove unwanted or unfashionable body and facial hair. Examples of such tweezers in gold may be seen in the current exhibition, but other metals, including copper, were also used. It would seem but a single small step from club to hammer or from tweezers to tongs, but apparently it was never taken.

Let us turn now to some of the actual metal working techniques in use in ancient America. By and large, they are similar or even identical to those used—far earlier—in the Old World. Some of these techniques are exceedingly intricate and complex, leading a number of culture historians to speculate whether they were indeed independently invented in the New World—the view long held by most, but by no means all, American archaeologists—or whether the art of metal working may have reached the New World, along with some other traits, through contact with the Old across the Pacific.

Gold and the gold-copper alloy, known as *tumbaga*, were made in a number of different proportions. With *tumbaga*, most commonly 30% gold was mixed with 70% copper. The Indians also made objects of pure copper.

An excellent summary of metal working achievements in ancient America is that of Dudley T. Easby Jr. of the Metropolitan Museum, published in the October, 1956, issue of Natural History. Easby suggests that long before the working of metals into so many intricate and aesthetically pleasing shapes by the great variety of techniques mentioned above, there must have been crude experiments with cold hammering of virgin nuggets of gold.

One might speculate that perhaps someone once found a bit of pure gold, silver or copper and tried to shape it as he might a piece of flint. Instead of chipping, however, it was found soft and malleable, giving under the blow of the hammer stone, rather than chipping. (It is actually possible to beat gold leaf as thin as 1/28,000 of an inch, and, as S. K. Lothrop, a veteran student of the metal working techniques of pre-Columbian America, has pointed out, a single grain of gold can be made to cover eighty square inches!)

Nevertheless, it is easy to underestimate the difficulties attendant to developing a true metal working technology from a hypothetical beginning such as attempts to chip nuggets of gold. What, for example, happens to a gold ingot when it is hammered? As Easby states, it soon becomes springy and unworkable, by a process known as "strain hardening." Today, we know that this is caused by changes in the micro-structure of the metal as it is being hammered. The pre-Columbian goldsmith could have had no such knowledge—all he knew was that his hammer simply bounced off the metal without affecting its shape. The harder the blow, the more brittle the metal becomes, and eventually this results in cracking.

The answer to this problem lies in a process known as annealing. If strain-hardened metal is heated, it loses its hardness and again becomes easy to work. This process, however, must be repeated again and again during the work, because renewed hammering will, of course, again lead to strain-hardening. And this technique of annealing is precisely that utilized by the ancient American metal worker, as it also was in the Old World. Hardening by hammering may, of course, be desired, and many objects formed by repeated hammering and annealing will actually be deliberately hammer-hardened as the final step to make them strong and springy. In addition to gold ornaments, weapons and tools of bronze and copper were tempered by hammer-hardening in both the Old and the New Worlds.

It should be pointed out, however, that there are a great many more technical problems attached to annealing. For one thing, the metal worker had to be extremely careful to remove the object from the fire at precisely the right moment to prevent the metal from melting. Gold, for example, gives almost no warning of color change before reaching its melting point (1063.0°C.), and Easby points out that even today gold is often annealed only in dark corners so that the smith can spot the subtle color change to dull red in time to withdraw it from the fire.

There is still another problem — that involving the formation of copper oxide scale on the surface of copper-gold, or copper-silver, alloy objects heated in the open air. Such scale must be removed, or the piece becomes unworkable. Today's craftsmen do this with a mild acid bath in a process known as "pickling," and it so happens that the ancient Indian metal worker did much the same, using organic acids won from certain plants. This also led to the use of the technique known as *mise en couleur*. The goldsmith learned that by alternately heating and pickling an object of silver-copper or gold-copper alloy, he could color the surface through concentrations of the precious metal. "The repeated action of forming and dissolving the copper oxide without affecting the gold or silver in the alloy," Easby writes, "left a surface richer in gold or silver each time it was carried out."

Martin Fernández de Enciso, speaking in 1519 of the Tairona of Colombia, said, "...the Indians owned much gold and copper. They had much gilded gold-copper alloy. They gild the copper with an herb whose juices, when applied, remove oxidized copper, leaving a surface of pure gold."

Gold does not oxidize; copper does, and so can be removed from the surface of an alloyed piece as we have just seen. The Spanish conquerors were naturally furious when deceived by this technique.

The best first-hand account of pre-Columbian metal working has come down to us thanks to the monumental work of that remarkable sixteenth century ethnographer, Fray Bernadino de Sahagún, whose Florentine Codex, or, more accurately, *Historia general de las cosas de Nueva España*, constitutes a veritable gold mine of information on the social, political, economic and religious life of Aztec Mexico before the Spanish Conquest. Until recently, this rich material was available only to those willing, and able, to struggle through the original Aztec (the Codex is a phonetic transliteration of spoken Aztec) or a Spanish translation; today, we are fortunate to have an excellent, complete English version by Arthur J. O. Anderson and Charles E. Dibble, published by the School of American Research in Santa Fe, New Mexico, and the University of Utah.

Gold working did not appear in Mexico until relatively late, apparently no earlier than the Toltec era, after about 900 A.D., or between fifteen to seventeen centuries later than in Peru. Nevertheless, once the techniques of metal working had become known

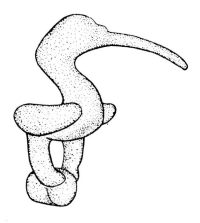

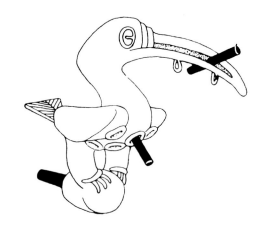

1. This rough core, made of clay mixed with charcoal, will be broken up and removed after casting, leaving the piece hollow inside. This saves gold and also permits the making of hollow vessels.

2. The rough core is first covered with a uniform coating of wax. The eyes, talons, suspension rings under the bill, and decorative holes have been added in the form of wax threads. The founder finishes the details of the wax model with sharp tools. The three black bars are the pegs to keep the core from slipping out of position during the work.

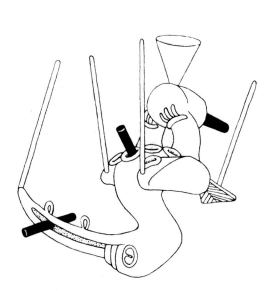

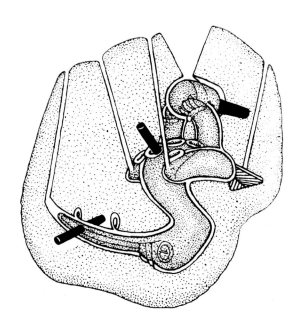

3. The casting will be done in an inverted position. Before enveloping the model in clay, a cone of wax is added to provide a pouring channel. And four wax rods have been added to provide air vents when the metal is poured in.

4. This drawing represents a section through the mold after the wax model has been melted out. The colored portion shows where the gold will flow between the shell and the core. It will rise into the air vents to form rods that will be later cut off and burnished. The core is finally broken and removed through the hollow bill and the holes in the breast and the back of the perch.

After Dudley T. Easby, Jr., Natural History, October 1956.

through diffusion from the south, Mexican craftsmen, particularly the Mixtecs of the Oaxaca area, perfected their art to such an extent that their jewelry — what little is known — seems in many respects technically and (at least to our eyes) aesthetically superior to much Central or South American gold.

The techniques, as stated, diffused to Mexico from the south, and Father Sahagún's account of the so-called "lost wax" casting of solid and hollow objects therefore holds true not only for Aztec Mexico but for South America as well. Indeed, it is remarkable that the process in both areas is very much the same as that developed in the ancient Near East around 3000 B.C., diffused from there over much of the Old World, and, in fact, still utilized today by both goldsmiths and dentists.

Father Sahagún's account, incidentally, is almost detailed enough to serve as a textbook introduction to lost wax casting.

Briefly, the process as described in Chapters 15 and 16 of Book 9 of the Florentine Codex is as follows:

The craftsmen, who were true professionals and whose tutelary deity was Xipe Totec, God of Spring and Renewal, first of all fashioned a model of the desired object in a mixture of powdered charcoal and potter's clay.

"If it were, perchance, a turtle," writes Sahagún, "just so was the charcoal (and clay core) modelled: its shell in which it can move; its head which is peering forth from it; its neck, which is moving; and its feet, which are as though extending.

"Or if a bird were to be fashioned of gold, just so was the charcoal (and clay) core carved, just so was it shaped, to give it feathers, wings, tail, feet."

Once the core had been carved to the artist's satisfaction, beeswax was melted and mixed with resin. This mixture was purified by straining, until all foreign matter had been removed. The wax was rolled out on a smooth stone by means of a wooden roller into a thin, even sheet, which was then placed over the entire surface of the carved and modelled core. The wax was carefully pressed into all carved areas and excess was pared and trimmed with a small knife. Decorative details were added in wax. Then, writes Sahagún, a paste of water and finely pulverized charcoal was evenly spread over the entire surface. (The latter, according to Easby, is accepted foundry practice today, except that an aqueous emulsion of graphite, instead of charcoal, is used.)

The next step was to enclose the entire piece in another mixture of clay and charcoal, this time of a coarser grain, forming a mold, with air vents and channel added for the pouring process. After it had dried for two days, the mold with its wax-and-charcoal-coated core inside was pre-heated, both to melt out the wax (hence the term "lost wax") and to dry the mold thoroughly before pouring in the molten gold, which could then flow freely and spread out evenly in the space left by the "lost wax" between the core model and the charcoal paste coating on the inside of the mold. After cooling, the mold was opened and the finished piece removed. The charcoal and clay core on the inside was then pulverized and removed through an opening, leaving the object hollow. The outer surface was burnished, washed and treated with such substances as powdered alum.

"Later," writes Sahagún, "it was made like flint, to finish it off, so that at last it glistened, it shone, it sent forth rays."

Easby, in his description of pre-Columbian gold working, adds that of course something had to be done to prevent the carved and modelled core from slipping out of position after the wax was melted out and before it was replaced by the molten gold. The ancient goldsmith accomplished this by piercing the wax-coated model with fine wooden pegs or maguey cactus spines which penetrated into the core and whose projecting ends were embedded in the outer shell to hold the core in place. Easby's simplified version of the steps used in casting a hollow bird ornament similar to those on view in the current exhibition is reproduced on the following page.

Such were some of the techniques used to produce the remarkable works on view in the current exhibition. Although representing but a fraction of what has been found, they give us some idea of what the great cultures of the Americas might have had to offer, had they not been snuffed out by the Conquest, and, indeed, what we might still gain from the heritage of the pre-Columbian past. Not in a material sense; for to class these objects of gold strictly under the heading of "material culture" as opposed to that of the spirit would be to fall precisely into the same trap as the Spaniards, who viewed it all as just so much loot, to be melted down into bullion.

We may be not able to recapture the sacred aura which once surrounded the precious metal, but we can appreciate beauty, and beauty is a thing of the spirit. The Spaniards, too, appreciated its beauty, though unfortunately not enough to prevent its destruction.

BIBLIOGRAPHY

EASBY, DUDLEY, T., JR.
1956 Sahagún reviviscit in the Gold Collections of the University Museum, University Museum Bulletin. Vol. 20, No. 3, September, 1956:3–15.
1956 Ancient American Goldsmiths. Natural History, Vol. 65, October, 1956:401–408.
LOTHROP, SAMUEL K.
1937 Coclé: An archaeological study of Central Panama. Part I. Peabody Museum Memoirs, Vol. 7, Cambridge, Mass.
1938 Inca Treasure as Depicted by Spanish Historians. The Southwest Museum, Los Angeles.
1941 Gold Ornaments of Chavin Style from Chongoyape, Peru. American Antiquity, 1941, No. 3:250–262.
1951 Gold Artifacts of Chavin Style. American Antiquity, No. 3, January 1951:226–240.
ROOT, WILLIAM C.
1949 Metallurgy. In: Handbook of South American Indians, Vol. 5:205–225. Bureau of American Ethnology, Bulletin 143. Washington, D.C.

Color Plates

This catalog makes no attempt to list all of the objects in the exhibition. The color plate numbers in no way correspond with exhibition numbers. The numbers listed at the end of each caption are the lending museums' designated numbers for the particular objects.

Plate 1 (and Back Cover).
The finest emerald crystal from the Banco de la República collection is this 1759 carat crystal of exceptional color and form. The crystal measures 5.0 x 4.5 x 8.9 cm.

Figure 1.
Guaqueros working and sorting the stream gravels for emeralds at Muzo, Colombia about 100 kilometers north of Bogotá.

Plate 2. (Left).
Four of the five Muzo mine crystals housed in the Banco de la República, Bogotá, Colombia. These crystals range in weight from 220 carats to 1796 carats and must be considered the largest fine Colombian emeralds in the world.

Plate 3. (Right).
Typical emeralds in matrix from the Muzo mine, characteristically consisting of black carbonaceous shale and white calcite.

Plate 4.
The first emerald crystal ever recovered from the Chivor mine in Colombia is the 632 carat "Patricia" emerald. The crystal is from the American Museum of Natural History, New York.

Plate 5.
This very fine 217.8 carat carved emerald is named the "Mogul" because it was carved by Mogul craftsmen in India in the 17th century. The emerald has typically Mogul floral motif carving on one side with Arabic calligraphy on the reverse. The Mogul emerald is courtesy of Allan Caplan, New York.

Plate 6. (Left).
One of the most spectacular pieces of historical emerald jewelry is this 300-year-old Spanish Inquisition Necklace from the Smithsonian Institution. The necklace contains 360 diamonds and 16 fine emeralds. It was reportedly worn in both the Spanish and French courts.

Plate 7. (Above).
The 75-carat "Hooker" emerald brooch is from the gem collection of the Smithsonian Institution. The emerald is remarkably free from the usually characteristic flaws and was purported to have been originally worn in the belt buckle of a sultan.

Figure 2.
An overview of the working at the Chivor mines seventy-five kilometers northeast of Bogotá.

Plate 8.
This magnificent 215.72 carat emerald cabachon measures 43 x 36 mm and was purported to have been presented to Ferdinand de Lesseps upon his completion of the Suez Canal in 1869, by the Khedive Ismāil Pasha. Courtesy of M. S. Sater & Company, Inc., Beverly Hills, Calif.

Plate 9.
Tairona pendant, bird. Cast and gilded
tumbaga. Bahía de la Traca, Santa Marta,
Magdalena. Height 6 cm. Museo del Oro 9026.

Plate 10.
Tairona bird pectoral. Hammered gold. Alto
Buriticá, Magdalena. Height 10.4 cm. Museo
del Oro 24.346.

Plate 11.
Lime-flask. Cast gold. A classic Quimbaya piece. Typically, the figure is nude except for ornaments and jewelry. In her hands she holds a pair of vessels of the kind which figure in the Treasure of the Quimbayas. Suspension loop on the head. Hacienda Las Margaritas, Sevilla, Valle del Cauca. Height 11.4 cm. Museo del Oro 21.212.

Plate 12.
Tairona bells. *Left:* Gilt *tumbaga;* hollow cast. The head may represent an alligator. San Pedro de la Sierra, Ciénaga, Magdalena. Height 4.6 cm. Museo del Oro 14.855. *Right:* Cast and gilded *tumbaga.* Human figure. Canaveral, Santa Marta, Magdalena. Height 3.4 cm. Museo del Oro 22.640.

Plate 13 (Overleaf).
Tairona nose ornament. Cast gold. Minca, Santa Marta, Magdalena. Width 8.9 cm. Museo del Oro 11.683.

Plate 14.
Pendant, male figure with head-dress. Cast
gold. Height 11.6 cm. Museo del Oro 6417.

Plate 15.
Sinú staff head, bird. Gold; hollow cast.
Sinú river area, Córdoba. Length 7.9 cm.
Museo del Oro 6378.

Plate 16.
Pectoral; disc with human figure. Hammered and repoussé gold. Diameter 14.5 cm. Museo del Oro 1899.

Plate 17.
Left: **Shell pendant.** Cast gold. Length 5.6 cm. Museo del Oro 6463. *Center:* **Shell (?).** Cast and surface-enriched *tumbaga.* Length 13.7 cm. Museo del Oro 6035. *Right:* **Fish or shell form.** Cast gold. Length 8.5 cm. Museo del Oro 3098.

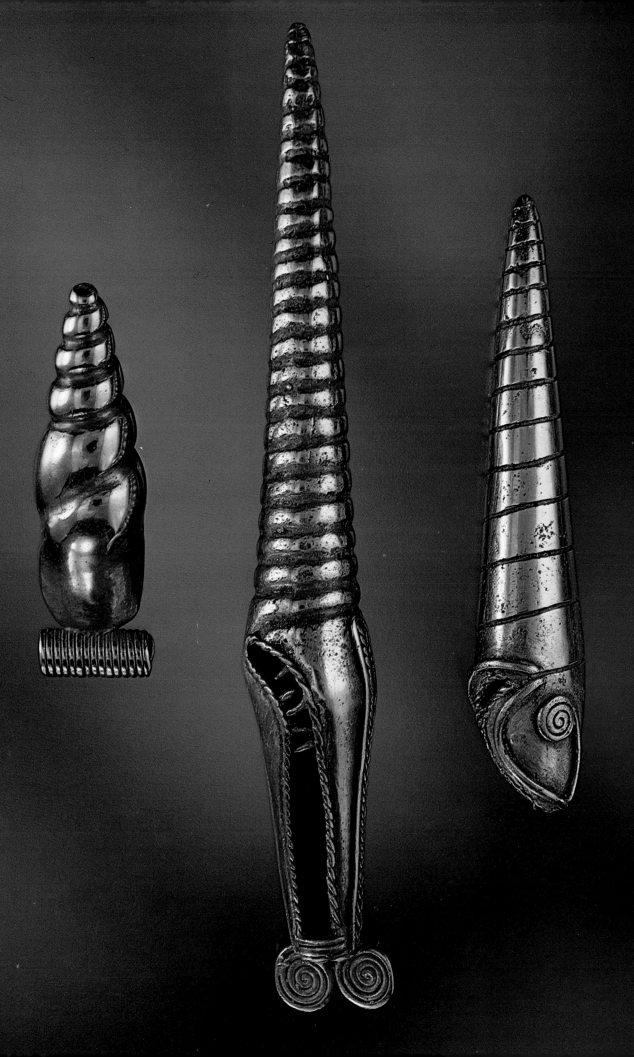

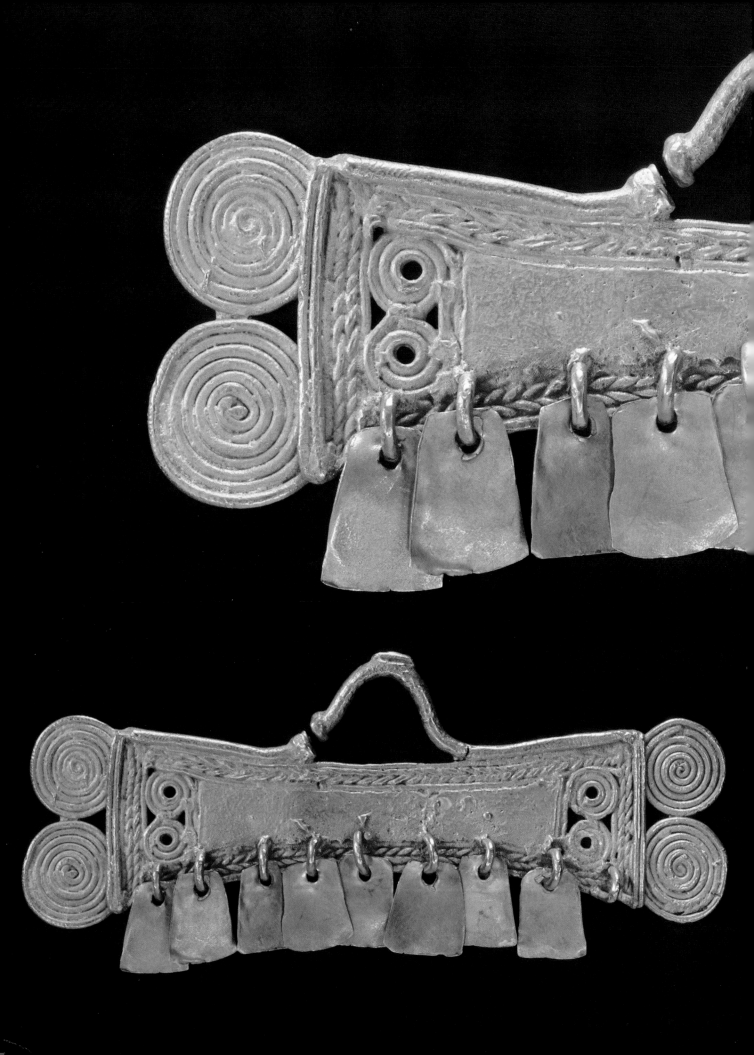

Plate 18. (Above).
Bell, shaped like a human head. Cast gold.
The headdress incorporates two bird heads.
There are two similar bells from San Marcos,
Bolivar, in the Sinú zone (Pérez de Barradas
1966, I:154). Height 4.7 cm. Museo del Oro
6513.

Plate 21 (Overleaf).
Sinú nose ornament. Cast gold. Made by
the false filigree process with wax wire, and
cast in a single operation. Sinú, Córdoba.
Width 13.7 cm. Museo del Oro 6953.

Plate 19. (Right).
Tairona necklace. Cast and gilded *tumbaga*.
Twenty-two frogs and twenty-six carnelian
beads. Minca, Santa Marta, Magdalena.
Length of largest frog 2.8 cm. Museo del Oro
12.549. *In Center:* **Frog pendant.** Gold, open-
backed casting. El Anclar, Montelibano, Córdoba. Length 2.6 cm. Museo del Oro 24.392.

Plate 20. (Left).
Sinú nose ornament. Cast gold; the scar on
top of the hook marks the end of the channel
through which the metal entered during casting. Between Ovejas and Carmen de Bolivar.
Width 10.9 cm. Museo del Oro 24.285.

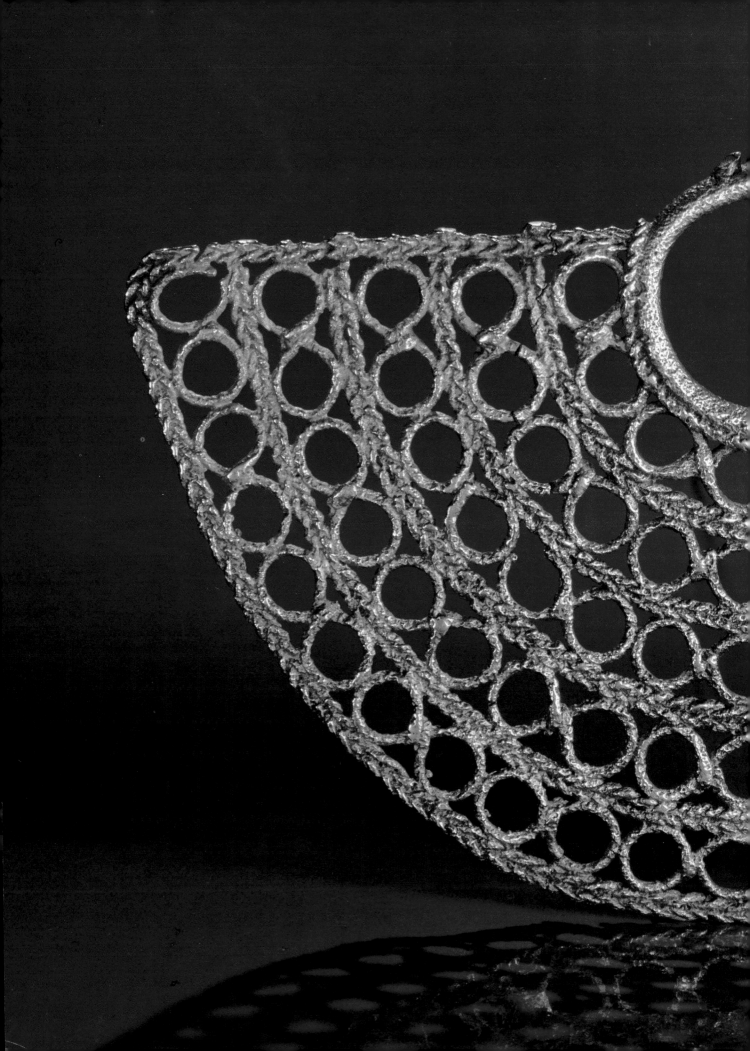

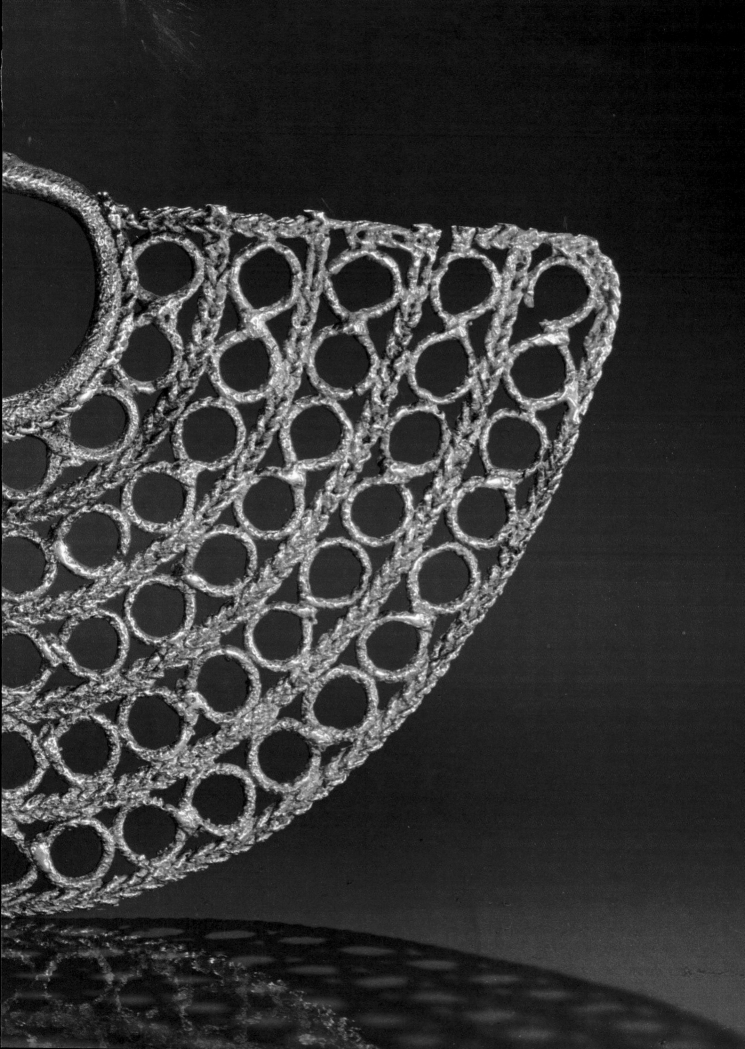

Plate 22.
Left: **Muisca tunjo, male figure with crown.** Cast *tumbaga.* El Chocho, Fusagasugá, Cundinamarca. Height 13.4 cm. Museo del Oro 6307. *Right:* **Muisca tunjo.** Cast *tumbaga.* In his right hand the figure holds a lime-flask and stick; in his left hand he carries a cup or dish. On his back is a shield. Castellanos notes that Muisca men were buried with their coca bags and lime-gourds. Pasca, Cundinamarca. Height 7.9 cm. Museo del Oro 25.614.

Plate 23.
Left to right: **Lime-dipper, with bird.** Cast gold. Restrepo, Valle del Cauca. Length 17.7 cm. Museo del Oro 13.365. **Lime-dipper, masked figure.** Cast gold. The mask, hair style and ear plugs resemble those of certain San Agustin sculptures (cf. Reichel-Dolmatoff 1972, pl. 46). There is another figure on the reverse. Campohermoso, Ataco, Tolima. Early Calima style. Length 31.4 cm. Museo del Oro 5857. **Lime-dipper, funnel-shaped head.** Cast gold. Length 16.5 cm. Museo del Oro 5762. **Lime-dipper, with masked figure holding a staff.** Cast gold. The mask, staff, the fan-shaped object in the left hand, and the *alter ego* animal figure behind the shoulders can all be matched in San Agustín statuary. Finca Grecia, Restrepo, Valle del Cauca. From an Early Calima grave. Length 30 cm. Museo del Oro 26. **Lime-dipper surmounted by a human figure.** Cast gold. Technologically, this item is a miniature *tour de force.* The figure is only 2.5 cm high, but the loin-cloth, crown and pendant are shown in detail, and there is a movable ring through the nose. One hand holds a transverse knife with a suspension loop; the other grasps a staff-like object with a dangling chain. Attached to the back is a funnel-shaped element with a perforated stone bead secured by a loop of twisted wire. Two concave ear discs, like the full-size examples from Calima graves, are attached at the shoulders by wire. Restrepo, Valle deCauca. Early Calima style. Length 25.8 cm. Museo del Oro 24.828.

Plate 24.
Tairona figure pendant. Cast and gilded *tumbaga.* He wears a bird headdress and a range of Tairona jewelry: crescentic ear ornaments, nose bar and necklace. Height 13.3 cm. Collection: Natural History Museum of Los Angeles County L.2100P.5.67-1.

Plate 25.
Left: **Tairona figure pendant.** Cast *tumbaga.* The figure wears the typical range of Tairona gold jewelry: diadem, crescentic earrings, double-bar nose ornament, and lip plug. All these categories are documented by numerous archaeological specimens. Minca, Santa Marta, Magdalena. Height 6.4 cm. Museo del Oro 11.445. *Right:* **Tairona figure pendant.** Cast and gilded *tumbaga.* The headdress incorporates two bats. Tairona region. Magdalena. Height 4.2 cm. Museo del Oro 22.802.

Plate 26.
Nose ornament. Sheet gold. The decorative
border and the three creatures are worked
from the rear and drawn freehand. Restrepo,
Valle del Cauca. Early Calima style. Width
17.3 cm. Museo del Oro 5376.

Plate 27.
Diadem. Cut and embossed sheet gold. The
nose ornament and ear discs are stapled to
the human face that forms the centrepiece.
The decorative detail is embossed from the
back and chased on the front. Hacienda
Calima, Valle del Cauca. Early Calima style.
Height 31 cm. Museo del Oro 4833.

Plate 28.
Tairona pendant, double-headed animal. Cast *tumbaga.* Bellavista, Magdalena. Length 7.1 cm. Museo del Oro 24.274.

Plate 29.
Top: **One of a pair of crescent ear ornaments.** Cast and hammered gold. Ornamented with human figures and the usual Nariño monkeys. Consacá, Nariño. Capulí period. Width 13.7 cm. Museo del Oro 25.218/9.
Bottom: **One of a pair of circular ear ornaments, with monkeys.** Cast and hammered gold. Córdoba, Nariño. Capulí period. Diameters 9.8, 10 cm. Museo del Oro 25.204/5.

Plate 30.
Pair of ear ornaments, with human heads. Gold; hammered and repoussé. Consacá, Nariño. Capulí period. Width 10.4 cm. Museo del Oro 25.212/3.

Plate 31. (Left).
Muisca tunjo, seated man. Cast gold. Height 5 cm. Museo del Oro 1263.

Plate 32. (Right).
Jaguar pendant (side and frontal views). Cast gold. El Banco, Magdalena. Length 12.1 cm. Museo del Oro 17.170.

Plate 33. (Left).
Darien pectoral. Cast *tumbaga* (60.4% gold,
18.8% copper, 18.4% silver). The figure has a
human body (with belt and breast ornament),
but a snouty, alligator-like face. The so-called
Darien pectorals are described in the
Schultes-Bright essay in the catalog. Corregi-
miento La María, Ansermanuevo, Valle del
Cauca. Height 7 cm. Museo del Oro 3492.

Plate 34. (Top Right).
One of a pair of circular openwork pendants.
Cast gold. Ubaque, Cundinamarca. Height
12.8 cm. Museo del Oro 7245/6.

Plate 35. (Bottom Right).
Pectoral disc, with embossed lizard. Hammered *tumbaga.* Diameter 16.2 cm. Museo
del Oro 66.

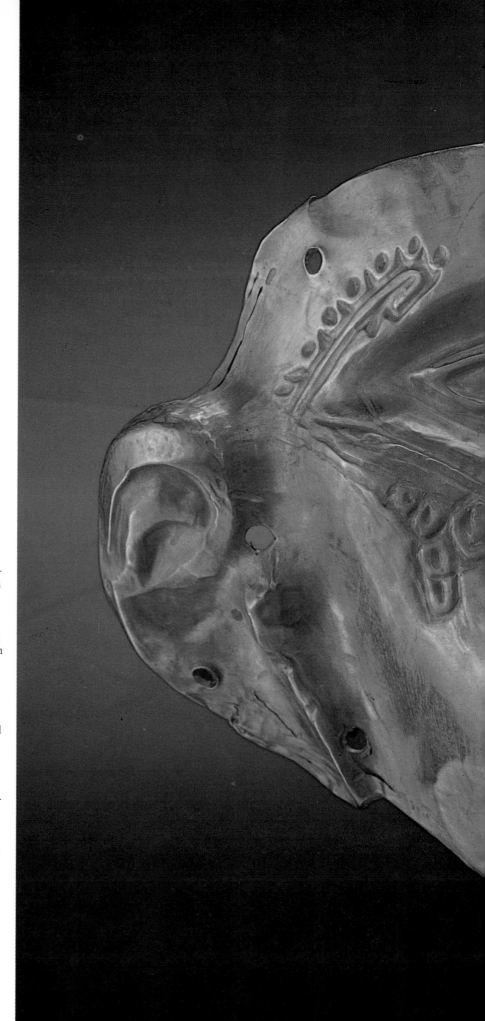

Plate 36.
Mask (also Catalog Cover).
Gold-rich *tumbaga*, with further surface
enrichment. This item is a masterpiece of
repoussé metalwork, and must once have covered a hollow-backed wooden mask to which
it was attached by pins through the large
holes at the sides and top. On the reverse of
the face, the metal was folded around the
edges of the underlying wooden mask, giving
some idea of its profile. The processes used in
making the gold mask can be reconstructed:
(1) The *tumbaga* sheet was prepared, and the
surfaces were enriched before being placed
over the backing (since both faces have been
pickled). (2) The wooden mask served as a
form or template, over which the sheet metal
was worked into shape. The metal split at
two points (below the chin and beside the
left temple). The damage was repaired by
overlapping the edges of the metal and pin-
ning through them into the underlying wood.
At certain points, the metal creased or puck-
ered, and these flaws are still visible on the
reverse. (3) Once the gold was plugged per-
manently to its backing, the outside face was
given a final burnish to remove all blemishes.
This process caused a slight ridging of the
metal against the heads of the nails (see the
hole at the right temple). Near Páez, Cauca
(in the Tierradentro region). Found in 1976
in a tomb with other objects, including fragments of a second mask, and also a large
sheet ornament with an embossed lizard
(now in the Museo del Oro). Width 12.5 cm.
Collection: Hernán Borrero Urrutia, Bogotá.

84

Plate 37.
Tolima pendant, fantastic animal. Solid, cast gold. Campohermoso, Ataco, Tolimo. Length 6.5 cm. Museo del Oro 5870.

Plate 38.
Tolima pectoral. Cast gold; hammer finished. Height 19 cm. Museo del Oro 4661.

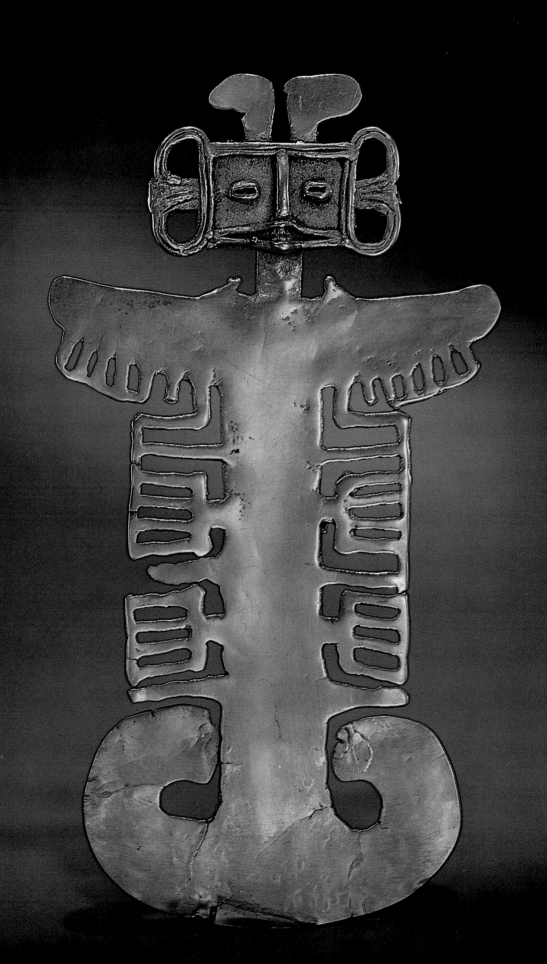

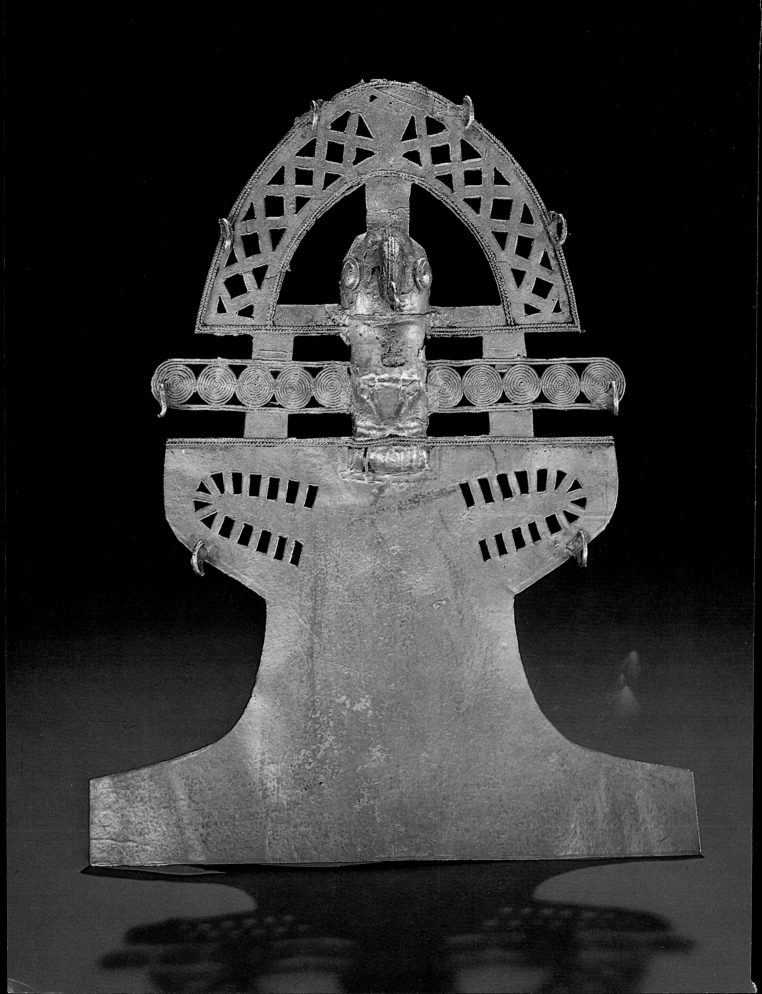

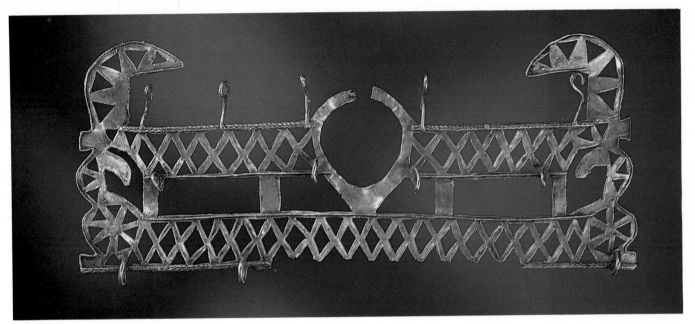

Plate 39. (Left).
Muisca bird pectoral. Gold-rich *tumbaga*;
cast. From the rear, the technique of manufacture can be clearly seen. The base plate,
openwork crescent, spiral strip and the bird
itself were made as four separate elements at
the wax stage (the bird by the matrix technique). These were assembled into a single
wax model and cast in one operation (Pérez
de Barradas 1958, I:182). Neighborhood of
Tunja, Boyacá. Height 14.7 cm. Museo del
Oro 6256.

Plate 40.
Openwork Muisca nose ornament. Cast
tumbaga. Ferrería, Pacho, Cundinamarca.
Width 20.2 cm. Museo del Oro 252.

Plate 41.
Muisca nose ornament, with two birds. Cast
and gilt *tumbaga.* Cueva de Vélez, Santander
del Sur. Width 12.1 cm. Museo del Oro 24.244.

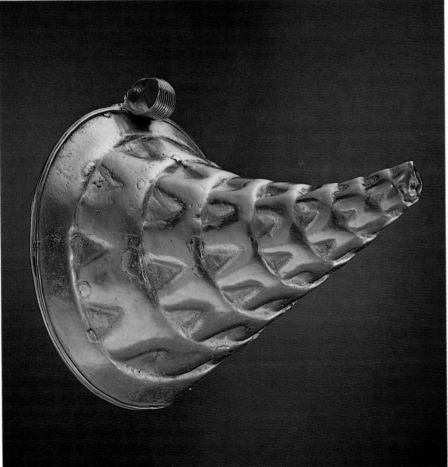

Plate 42. (Top Left).
Tweezers, with human figure. Cast and gilt *tumbaga.* The figure wears a headdress and earrings. The tweezers have a suspension loop at the top. Department of Quindío. Height 4.1 cm. Museo del Oro 3061.

Plate 43. (Bottom Left).
Penis cover *(lower left).* Cast gold. The inside is interesting for the information it gives about the preparation of the clay core before this was covered with wax prior to casting. The sides of the triangles, and also the base lines on which they stand, were deeply inscribed in the core material; then the clay was removed from the triangular areas thus delineated. The detail is much less sharp on the outer surface. Bartolomé de Las Casas describes the use of penis covers among the Indians of Sinú-Urabá: *"They walked about... in their bare skins as they were accustomed to in their own land, their shameful parts enclosed in tubes of gold shaped like funnels."* The loop allows the object to be tied to a cord around the waist. The unimpressive size of this specimen may arouse doubts about its function as a penis sheath, but there are other (and larger) ones from the Sinú region on which either the testicles or the glans are indicated. Majagual, Sucre. Length 10.3 cm. Museo del Oro 7508.

Plate 44. (Right).
Left to right: **Alligator pendant.** Cast gold. Length 7.9 cm. Museo del Oro 5928. **Pendant with spiral ornaments.** Open-backed casting; gilt *tumbaga.* Probably Quimbaya zone. Length 14.1 cm. Museo del Oro 6034. **Lizard pendant.** Cast and gilt *tumbaga.* Suspension loop behind head. Probably Quimbaya zone. Length 11.6 cm. Museo del Oro 8138.

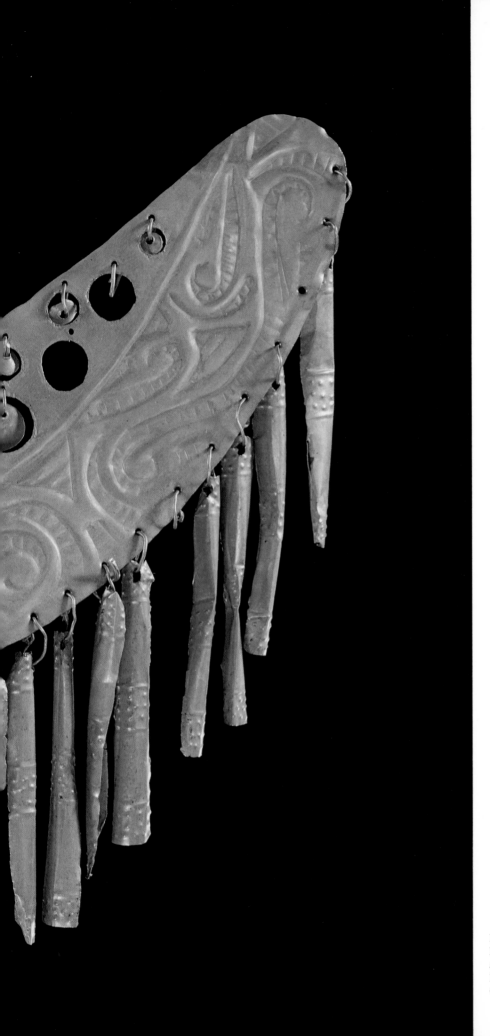

Plate 45.
Nose ornament with pendants. Hammered
and repoussé gold. Restrepo, Valle del Cauca.
Early Calima style. Width 18 cm. Museo del
Oro 6287.

Plate 46.
Large hollow figure. Pottery; traces of orange paint on the torso. Holes in the bottoms of the feet allowed the steam to escape, thus preventing shattering at the firing stage. The personage wears a necklace, wrist band, nose stud and ear plug. Holes around the edges of the ears may once have held gold rings. The skull is artificially deformed. Tumaco style. Height 67.5 cm. Museo Arqueológico del Banco Popular, Bogotá. T-12384.

Plate 47.
Group of three solid figures. Pottery. Each is made from a slab of clay to which the limbs are added. These square, solid figures always consist of nude males (usually seated), with holes of unknown function in the heads and bodies. The noses are perforated for the insertion of metal ornaments. Most of these figures come from the Department of Caldas, within the Quimbaya zone. AD 1200 to Spanish Conquest (Bruhns 1976: 150–5). (418) Rioblanco, El Cairo, Valle del Cauca. Height 20 cm. Museo del Oro CQ-2938. (419) Quimbaya, Quindio. Height 20.9 cm. Museo del Oro CQ-3715. (420) Rioblanco, El Cairo, Valle del Cauca. Height 18 cm. Museo del Oro CQ-2942.

Plate 48.
Lime-container. Heavy sheet gold with
repoussé ornament. The object was made
as two hemispherical units, joined around
the "equator." Height 7.6 cm. Museo del
Oro 5563.